# BRINGING UP PARENTS

## The Teenager's Handbook

## by Alex J. Packer, Ph.D.

### Edited by Pamela Espeland
### Illustrated by Harry Pulver, Jr.

free spirit
PUBLiSHiNG®

Works
for kids™

**Library of Congress Cataloging-in-Publication Data**

Packer, Alex J.

    Bringing up parents : the teenager's handbook / Alex J. Packer : illustrated by Harry Pulver, Jr.

        p.   cm.

    Includes index.

    Summary: Discusses ways that teenagers can improve their relationship with their parents and help each other develop mutual trust and respect.

    ISBN 0-915793-48-2

    1. Parent and teenager—Juvenile literature. 2. Conflict of generations—Juvenile literature. 3. Interpersonal relations—Juvenile literature. 4. Family—Juvenile literature. [1. Parent and child. 2. Conduct of life.] I. Pulver, Harry, ill. II. Title.

HQ799.15.P33  1993

306.874—dc20                             92-36625

                                               CIP

                                               AC

Cover and book design by MacLean and Tuminelly

Illustrations by Harry Pulver, Jr.

Index prepared by Eileen Quam and Theresa Wolner

10 9 8

Printed in the United States of America

FREE SPIRIT PUBLISHING INC.

400 First Avenue North, Suite 616

Minneapolis, MN 55401

(612) 338-2068

For my own parents,
who have turned out
quite nicely, thank you.

# Acknowledgments

*I am deeply grateful to the following individuals who helped to make this book possible:*

*Josh Horwitz, for putting me in touch with the right people;*

*Gail Ross, my agent, and Elaine English, for their generously given advice and support;*

*Judy Galbraith, for her enthusiasm and flexibility;*

*Pamela Espeland, for her sensitive and sensible editing; and finally,*

*All the children and parents whose insight and example inspired the ideas in this book.*

# CONTENTS

# READ THIS FIRST!

This book can provide you with new insights and skills.  It can give you tools and techniques to:

- increase your freedom,
- become more independent,
- have greater influence in family decisions,
- gain new privileges,
- head off problems before they happen, and
- break destructive cycles.

It can offer you strategies for bringing up parents who will:

- trust you,
- let you correct your own mistakes,
- listen to what you say and respect your opinions, and
- accept your feelings.

This book can help you discover:

- what makes your parents tick,
- how to use "parent psychology" to get what you want and need,
- how to solve problems and lessen conflict,
- how to avoid getting backed into a no-win corner, and
- what to do when your parents are unreasonable and unfair.

This book lays out a smorgasbord of strategies.  What happens after that is up to *you*.  It's up to your motivation, creativity, flexibility, and commitment.  If changes occur, if miracles are wrought, it will be because of you.

Only you can restore trust to your household, only you can maneuver your family to new attitudes, new approaches for decision-making and conflict-solving. Only you can choose the ideas most relevant to your parents, your problems, your purposes. Only you can prevent forest fires.

With this book, you can become a sculptor of family dynamics, an artist of human understanding and relationships. You'll have a palette of powers you can use to color your world with brighter hues. It's up to you to decide when to dip your brush into your trust fund, when to add a stroke of apology, a line of levity, a dab of tolerance, a wash of understanding. If the current picture of your family life is not a pretty one, throw it out. A new canvas awaits your masterful touch.

This book also assumes that your parents care about you. Probably they do, and you know that they do. Or probably they do, but you sometimes think that they don't (like after an argument or a big, fat NO!!!). Or maybe, sadly, they really don't. In which case, you might (logically) ask, "Why bother trying the strategies in this book? Won't I just be wasting my time?" And I might (reasonably) answer, "No, you won't be wasting your time. These strategies will still help you get through your teenage years with greater freedom, independence, influence, and self-respect. Any time you spend learning to get along better with others—and improving your chances of getting what you want—is time well spent. I promise!"

# NAME-CALLING

The term I use to refer to the adult(s) with whom you live should, ideally, recognize your particular domestic circumstance. However, if every time I mention these folks I have to say "your parents, or parent, or step-parents, or mother and stepfather, or adoptive father and girlfriend, or guardians, or foster mom," this book will be 4,000 pages long and by the time you finish reading it, you'll have teenage children of your own.

Therefore, on behalf of efficiency and reading ease, I will use the term "parents" as the label for whatever form of adult(s) you break bread with. It doesn't mean that I think you all live with that man and woman whose rousing acts of nature resulted in your arrival on the scene, nor does it mean that the ideas in this book are aimed at kids who live with two biological parents. The ideas in this book are aimed at kids who live with *people*. So, rest assured, this book will work for you whether you live with one, two, three, or more adults, whether your folks are divorced, remarried, unmarried, straight, gay, twice divorced, once removed, or three times separated and now living with your mother's fourth husband's parents' aunt's boyfriend.

This book also talks about people who are roughly between the ages of 12 and 17. Unfortunately, there doesn't seem to be a good word to describe those who inhabit this particular age range. What would you call them?

- "People-twelve-to-seventeen"? Awkward, and takes too long to say.
- "Adolescents"? Sounds like something you'd only touch with a pair of tweezers.
- "Kids"? Conceivable, but offensive to those who don't want to be associated with runny noses, skinned knees, and Kool-Aid.
- "Children"? Produces the fear that you're about to get a bath, receive a lecture, have your picture taken, or be sent to bed.
- "Boys"? Has the annoying tendency to overlook girls.
- "Girls"? Same problem in reverse.
- "Teens"? Only used by Madison Avenue when they want to sell to you, and by psychologists when they want to study you.

I think you can begin to see the problem. Isn't it interesting that a society that has a hard time finding a respectful place for people your age also has a hard time finding a respectful word for people your age? While stalking this perfect term to describe your condition, I will, most likely, end up using many of the above labels throughout this book. As far as I'm concerned, adolescents, kids, children, boys, girls, and teens are all wonderful folks. No matter what word I use, please know that it is meant to carry my respect and best wishes for this challenging time of your life.

# IF I CALLED THIS AN INTRODUCTION, YOU'D PROBABLY SKIP IT SO I WON'T AND YOU SHOULDN'T

I don't know the exact nature of problems you're having with your parents. I don't know whether you have occasional fights that interrupt good feelings or occasional good feelings that interrupt fights. I don't know whether you love and admire your parents or can't stand the sight of them. I don't know if your folks are too restrictive or too meek, if they over-parent or under-parent. I don't know if they're wise and wonderful saints, wishy-washy nerds, aging hippies, stern tyrants, well-meaning bumblers, or people preoccupied with troubles of their own. I don't know how you fit into the picture, or where you range on the scale from innocent victim to malicious monster.

Victim    OR    Monster

What I *do* know is that the very nature of adolescence and middle-aged parenthood sets the stage for family conflict, and that conflict, when not handled with care, can destroy trust, confidence, and family friendship.

Isn't it amazing; you need a license to fish, drive, fix teeth, and sell real estate, yet to be a parent, which is a lot harder, all you have to do is sit down and decide to have some kids. Unfortunately, the fact that your parents figured out how to bring you into the world doesn't mean they automatically know what to do now that you're here.

In spite of this, everyone still assumes that parents know best. They're the ones, so the legend goes, who control the family mood, who take the lead, who have the skill and insight to find solutions for family conflict.

Well, as I'm sure you've already discovered, that's simply not true. Parents don't always know how to solve problems. They don't always know how to reduce tension, communicate respectfully, or relate to their teenage children. Meanwhile, the family's out of control. Anger, argument, hurt, and mistrust—the tiniest spark can trigger an explosion of hostility. The air is often filled with tears and trauma, with name-calling and charges of bad attitude and irresponsible behavior.

Why does it have to be like this, you ask? It doesn't. If your parents, for whatever reasons, aren't taking the initiative to solve family problems, then you can be the one to do it.

It won't be easy. Bringing up parents during the adolescent years is a difficult, frustrating, and often thankless task, for this is the time when parents can seem distant, demanding, moody, or self-centered as they cope with the pressures of midlife. This is the time when financial insecurities, anxieties over aging, marital or sexual problems, stress from the workplace, and even (believe it or not) the responsibilities of children and family can make parents irritable, inconsistent, and unreasonable.

One minute they smother you with love, the next they can't be bothered. One minute they won't listen, the next they want to know e-v-v-v-v-erything. One minute it's YES, the next it's NO.

*"You're too old for this."*

*"You're too young for that."*

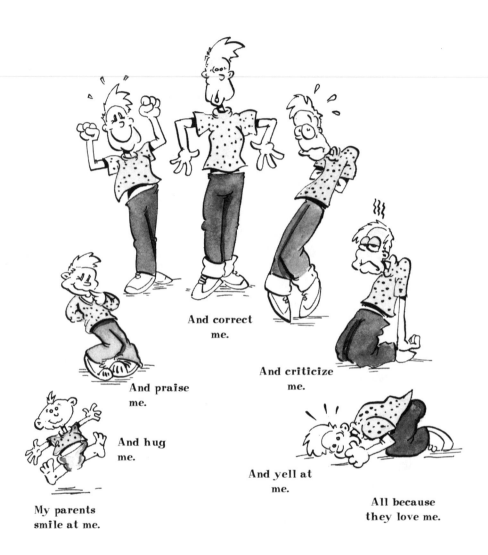

And correct
me.

And criticize
me.

And praise
me.

And hug
me.

My parents
smile at me.

And yell at
me.

All because
they love me.

Even the most tolerant and caring teenager may be tempted to throw in the towel and give up. Don't! With patience, humor, and a knowledge of the strategies in this book, you can help bring your parents through the adolescent years and make this a time of joy, warmth, and growth for them and you. You can learn to bring up parents who are more trusting, open-minded, and sensitive to your needs and feelings. You can bring up parents who will like you as well as love you, parents who will want to say...

*"Yes."*

*"Of course."*

*"Why, certainly."*

...instead of...

*"Forget it."*

*"Not a chance."*

*"Go to your room."*

In order to convey the concepts and strategies involved in bringing up parents, I have broken the process into many bite-sized chunks. Each chunk, each single technique, has its own value and can be put to immediate use. Because of this, you can read the book in any order and begin to reap the benefits.

Keep in mind, though, that whatever route you choose for traveling the paths of this book, it should cover all the territory. For it is only when you put the separate tactics together—when you get them inside of yourself as a way of being, when you build upon successes and mistakes to increase your skill and understanding—that you will be a true master of the art of parent-raising.

So take these ideas, these chunks: the insights, scoops, tricks, techniques, low-downs, high jinks, how-to's, why-fors, please do's, and don't-you-dares. Take them. Add milk, cocoa, and stir. Then drink in the pleasure of your new power—power to bring up parents who are considerate, understanding, and respectful; power to achieve that later curfew, that special permission, that extra privilege; power to bring up parents who are secure, sensitive, and mature; power to change your family and your life.

# NOTE FOR PARENTS

# Chapter One

# THE NATURE OF THE BEASTS

# PARENTS: CAN'T LIVE WITH 'EM, CAN'T LIVE WITHOUT 'EM

*Parents (Homo sapiens painus neckum).* In all the animal kingdom, it is hard to find a creature more proud, powerful, and predictably provocative than the Parent. Displaying a concern for their young that borders on the bothersome, members of this species have been observed exhibiting the following belittling behaviors towards offspring:

- They threaten.
- They order.
- They warn.
- They judge.
- They criticize.
- They preach.
- They lecture.

> *"Either that room gets cleaned up now, or else!"*
>
> *"Can't you do anything right?"*
>
> *"If I were you...."*
>
> *"When I was your age...."*
>
> *"How can you be so careless?"*
>
> *"You'll do as you're told."*

- They put you down.
- They humiliate.
- They prophesize.
- They nag.
- They accuse.
- They name-call.

*"You're acting like a baby."*

*"How can you be so stupid?"*

*"Don't you ever think of anyone except yourself?"*

*"You'll never amount to anything if you don't buckle down."*

- They shame.
- They coerce.
- They trivialize.
- They dash hopes.
- They interrogate.

*"Why don't you act your age?"*

*"If you know what's good for you...."*

*"Don't be silly."*

*"Where have you been?"*

They say one thing and do another. They tell you why you can't instead of how you might, what's wrong instead of what's right. And it's all done in the name of love:

*"For your own good."*

*"Because we care."*

*"Because we're your parents and we know what's best."*

Some of you may think I'm being a little hard on parents. Look, I don't have anything against parents. Some of my best friends are parents. I know that there have been sightings of parents engaged in joyful play and harmonious habitation with their children. I have been told of occasions when parents have lavished upon their progeny generous amounts of respect, encouragement, and junk food. I myself have witnessed those moments of glorious and uplifting familial warmth that can occur when parents convey love, understanding, and a bigger allowance upon their offspring.

So what do you want me to do? Write a book about how to get along with your parents when everything's just fine? About how to deal with the old man when he's fair, open-minded, and reasonable? You don't need to read that kind of book any more than I need to write it.

What you *do* need, though, is some help for those times when everything isn't just fine. When your parents are *not* fair, open-minded, and reasonable. When the weight of tension, conflict, and mistrust in your household threatens to crush everyone's spirit and self-esteem.

It's a funny thing in families: Often, the greater the love and commitment between family members, the greater the conflict and hurt. It's precisely because people care, because they want to protect and guide and make over those they love in their own image, that so many problems develop.

What do you care if some jerk at school criticizes the way you dress, or the lady down the street doesn't trust your judgment, or the gym teacher doesn't like your attitude? Big deal. But when it's your own family, your own parents, brothers, and sisters, you *do* care, deep down. You want their love, respect, and approval, and they want yours. You have an investment in each other that you don't want to lose. It's the caring that makes you fight, and the fighting that makes you feel you no longer care.

So you end up with this loving, caring family that's tearing itself apart with sniping, snapping, and battling. You may love each other, but you don't like each other. In fact, half the time you can't stand each other. This is the point so many families reach. This is the point at which so many families remain stuck; stuck, that is, until things get worse.

You, however, are already way ahead of the game. No matter how many problems you have with your parents, chances are that things can get better. Why? Because in reading this book, you've made a decision to try. That right there—just making a decision—sets you apart from most people.

Most kids deal with problems at home by fighting, arguing, and slamming doors. They run away, they lie, they cry, they avoid, they escape, they keep their hurt at bay with drugs or drinking. It may never occur to them that any of this could change. As the wounds of conflict deepen, these kids withdraw, give up, hate their parents, and, whether they know it or not, hate themselves.

No wonder it's so hard for them to imagine a life that's NEW and IMPROVED! A family spirit that's BIGGER, BOLDER, and BRIGHTER with love that will not fade!! A home that's 99 44/100 tension-free!!! It's hard to

imagine because kids are brought up believing that *parents* are supposed to solve problems. So what do you do when the people who are expected to solve the problem *are* the problem?

That's where you come in. If you don't like the way your parents are bringing you up, you're going to have to bring them up. You're going to have to show them how to be more mature, tolerant, and considerate. You're going to have to help them feel confident and good about themselves so they can feel good about you. It won't be easy; parents can be so resistant to change! You'll have to look at your own actions and attitudes as closely as theirs. But the increased trust, freedom, and acceptance your parents extend to you will be worth it.

Why am I so confident of your chances for success? I have four excellent reasons:

1. You, like most teenagers, are very sensitive to people's feelings, needs, and messages. You'll be able to put those skills to good use.

2. Many problems occur simply because no one tends to them. No one says, "Hey, here's a problem, let's solve it." You're willing to take the initiative to solve problems.

3. You're motivated. You're reading this book and are courageous enough to set a goal, no matter how scary it seems, to lead your family in a new direction.

4. The ideas in this book are good! They're based on reality, on human nature. They recognize what it's like to be a teenager or a parent. They respect the needs and feelings of all family members.

While there's a lot more I'd like to tell you about this book and the changes you'll be able to bring about in your family, heaven can wait. For now, let's get back to those bizarre birds who keep you under their wings: your parents.

You remember them—the creatures with eyes in the backs of their heads and the ability to read minds. They're the ones who, out of genuine love and concern for your well-being, can do so much damage. In order to bring them up in a new way, you've got to learn as much as you can about them, their habits, their feelings, and their points of view. You've got to understand how they see you, how they see themselves, and how they see their role as parents.

Naturally, your parents want you to be happy, healthy, brilliant, witty, mature, responsible, athletic, neat, attractive, successful, creative, honest, well-mannered, and socially adept. Is that all? No, not if your parents also

pressure you to excel. Then this modest set of expectations can only expand. All A's isn't good enough; if you're that smart, how about working harder to become valedictorian? You're athletic? Well, let's see some leadership—team captain, no less! You're college-bound? Could it mean anything that your mom grew ivy on the bars of your crib?

Parents can become so focused on what they want their child to become that they lose sight of what their child is, even who their child is. Should you be so lucky to reach one of their goals, well, that's what they expect from you. Your success is taken for granted, and whoosh, before you can say Harvard Law School, they've swooped in with their sights set on a new target.

Why can't they accept you for who you are? You'll never be the person they want you to be, so why can't they let you be yourself? Unfortunately, many parents judge their success as parents by the extent to which they can identify and correct "flaws" in their children. What happens, sadly, is the destruction of the parent-child relationship. Instead of a loving, flowing relationship between two equals (equals as human beings even if one has more experience or power than the other), you end up with a relationship based upon roles, where the parent is dominant and the child is inferior.

Once these roles are established, you can lose your identity. It's as if you become an object instead of a person, a lump of clay to be molded. Somehow in this "child role" you're made to feel less than equal, less than human, like a doll to be dressed and groomed in someone else's image. You lose your rights, you lose touch with your feelings, you become suspended between your parents' expectations and your true self. You become a son, a daughter, an investment, a chip off the old block, an ideal, a potential, a mirror, a dream, an extension. You become property, "my kid," something to be owned. You become everything except yourself.

Your parents, out of their love and concern, are doing what they believe is best, yet you feel attacked, mistrusted, misunderstood, and unloved. Their constant focus on the negative, on improving you, makes you think you're a failure.

You're going to be angry and defensive. You're going to want to strike back. How can you accept them if they won't accept you? A vicious cycle is established. The more your parents pick, nag, and scold, the more you annoy and reject them; the more you annoy and reject them, the more they pick,

nag, and scold. It no longer matters who started it; you're all stuck in a cycle of hurt and criticism that is likely to get worse.

Breaking this cycle and others like it will be one of your most valuable strategies for bringing up accepting and considerate parents. (More about that later.) For now, let's keep peeling away the protective layers that surround your parents and see what lies inside. How do they feel? Believe it or not (and you may prefer not to), your parents have many of the same feelings that you do.

Your parents, who seemingly have all the power, money, and independence, can also feel rejected, unloved, and unappreciated. They see themselves as the people who have done more for you than anyone. They got up in the middle of the night to feed and comfort you, they sacrificed many of their plans and purchases for your benefit. This makes them feel entitled to your obedience and appreciation.

When they don't get it, they feel resentful and hurt. They feel like they can't do anything right in your eyes; you've written them off as out of touch, narrow-minded, materialistic, and overly concerned with what people think. You don't want to be seen with them; you don't like how they drive, what they wear, what they value. And, because of the cycle of criticism already established in the household, you lose no opportunity to peddle your disdain in their direction.

They feel attacked, ignored, misunderstood, and abused. They feel that they're taken for granted, that they're seen as objects: handers-out of money, cookers of food, cleaners of the house, chauffeurs, protectors, tools, tutors. They feel stereotyped into the "parent role," and in that role they feel that they are less than equal. They feel that their children don't care about them, don't like them, and don't extend them courtesies that mere strangers would receive.

> *"Bull-oney!" you may say with less-than-correct spelling. "If they feel like that, it's their own fault. What do they expect? If they'd get off my case, I'd get off theirs."*

> *"Also," you may interject with less-than-correct grammar, "why should I treat them good if they don't treat me good?"*

That's a reasonable question. Look, the point is that a cycle of behavior has already been set. We've established that your parents haven't taken or won't take steps to break the cycle. That leaves you. Somebody has to be

willing to take chances, to attempt some bold, new tactics. Somebody has to be strong, wise, and adventurous. Sure, you can do nothing, you can lay all the blame at your parents' feet. But your life will still be miserable. You won't have the respect, freedom, and support you deserve.

Your goal is to change your parents' behavior and attitude towards you. Problem is, you can't change someone else's behavior and attitude very easily. Lord knows, your parents have been trying to do that with you, and look where it's gotten them! You can't force your parents to be a certain way any more than they can force you. What you *can* do, though, is act in a way that makes their attitude and behavior towards you obsolete, unnecessary, and unjustified. That is what will get them to change.

Now, this doesn't mean that you must become some goody-two-shoes, yes sir, thank you ma'am, I-think-I'll-go-wash-the-kitchen-floor-scrub-the-toilet-and-brush-my-teeth type of person. What it does mean is that you're in the driver's seat. You're going to make the first moves, call the shots, and be a model for your parents. How else are they going to learn?

You're going to do this to meet your own needs—for your own happiness, freedom, and rights as a human being. Your parents will become happier in their lives, too. If your anger at them is so great that the thought they might benefit along with you is too hard to swallow, well, there's not much I can do for you. I'd suggest you try to return this book or use it to prop open a window or steady an uneven table. However, if you *are* willing to share the health, it's going to mean breaking those patterns of behavior and thinking that cause so much pain and conflict.

Breaking cycles. It's like when you were a kid. Remember when someone took something of yours and wouldn't give it back? You, being a clever sort, immediately grabbed something you could hold hostage.

*"Give it back!"*

*"You give me mine and I'll give you yours."*

*"Uh-uh. I don't trust you. You give me mine first and then I'll give it back."*

*"No way, Ray."*

You're both stuck in this stalemate, this cycle of mistrust. Nobody's making a first move. So what do you do? Give up? Say goodbye to your belonging? Not if it's important to you. You might try to find another person, a neutral referee to whom you could both give the objects, who would then return them to their rightful owners. But what if no one else is around? Then what?

You only have two choices. You can continue the stalemate (where everybody loses), or you can take a chance by breaking the cycle. You can give the object back to the other person and hope that your act of courage and trust will be returned in kind. You're not doing it to be "nice," you're doing it for your own best interests, to get what is rightfully yours. Of course, you're taking a risk, and it might not work. But what do you have to lose? You've already lost the possession you seek to recover. You can't be any worse off than you already are.

It's the same in your own home. What do you have to lose by taking the initiative? There's already more than enough fighting and ill will to go around. Chances are that life can only get better, and it *will* get better as you replace negative cycles with positive ones. In order to do that, let's take another look at the old folks at home.

## 14 + 40 = Bad News

There are a lot of reasons parents and teenagers fight that have nothing to do with specific personalities and everything to do with the nature of being 14 and 40. Unfortunately, these generational or "life-stage" conflicts become personalized, adding more fuel to the fire of family feuding.

Many people assume (until they become one) that being an adult is a piece of cake. There's this magic moment, so the myth goes, when all of a sudden you are *grown up*, mature, together, fully aware of your needs and feelings. The doubts, fears, and confusions of adolescence disappear. In adulthood, you are confident and secure. You know who you are, what you want out of life, and where you're going.

Well, that's wrong. While adults certainly have their moments of serenity and even-keeled growth (just like you), there are other times when they can be plagued with worry, pain, and problems. One of those times, thanks to a cruel quirk of nature, often occurs during the period when parents have teenage children.

This phase, this midlife crisis (the name alone is enough to depress any self-respecting adult), is similar in many ways to adolescence. It's a time when your parents are examining their lives, their dreams, their relationships, and their values. It's a time when drastic change is possible, when careers and marriages come under a lot of pressure, when new roles and identities are considered or embraced. For some reason, instead of making your parents more understanding of you and your feelings, this time can make them less that way. Opposites attract and likes repel; in the metallurgy of family dynamics, it is *because* you and your parents share certain feelings and vulnerabilities that you get on each others' nerves.

During this period in your parents' lives, the mere fact that you're a teenager can serve to twist the knife of midlife evaluation and introspection they have placed in themselves. The bloom of your youth is a mirror to their advancing years. The extent to which they regret certain choices is the extent to which they may seek to control your choices. The degree to which they pick at you may reflect the degree to which they are jealous of you and your life as a teenager.

> *"Jealous of ME?  They're the ones with all the freedom.  Nobody tells them what to do.  What could they possibly be jealous of?"*

Well, they may be jealous of that which is adolescence. They may be jealous of your options. The world is a banquet of opportunities and experiences for you; life is a feast of possibilities and a buffet of choices. Your parents, however, have already made many of their choices. Patterns have been set, limits created. Their options are fewer.

They may be jealous of your dreams. While I hope all of your parents' dreams came true, chances are that the reality of life and the cold, cruel world have conspired to make them abandon many of their hopes. Your dad now recognizes that it's unlikely he'll ever be president of the company or quarterback for the New York Giants. Your mom sees the years pass by and with them her crack at being a concert pianist or chief of surgery at the hospital. Your parents may still be happy and feel blessed, but there could be a sigh of wistful envy (if not a snort of scorn) when they hear your great and ever-changing plans.

They may be jealous of your youthful looks and body. In spite of all that jogging, Dad's getting paunchier and his hair ain't what it used to be. You, however, are lean and taut, your Rock of Gibraltar stomach a mocking

reminder to Dad's sagging shoreline. You beat him at tennis and bear less than sympathetic witness to the huffing and puffing from his side of the net. Meanwhile, Mom's more wrinkled, the first signs of gray have dared to appear, and it seems the less she eats the more weight she gains. While Mom finds it harder and harder to fit into a size eight, neither pizza nor French fries keep you from looking fabulous in your bathing suit and summer scanties.

Even the raging rapids of teenage romance can make parents jealous; the grass is always greener, you know, and enough time has passed for them to have forgotten that along with the joy of first loves and first kisses can come anxiety, confusion, and hurt. Perhaps, looking from the sandbar of middle age, they yearn for another chance to experience those years of romantic and sexual discovery—a chance you are about to enjoy and they will never have again.

There's still more in your life to make your parents jealous. How about your friends, independence, and mobility compared to when they were kids? How about your freedom?

*"My freedom???!!! They don't let me do anything!"*

You may think that you have no freedom—that your parents don't let you do anything. And you may be right. But it's a different sort of freedom that your parents might envy. It's the freedom from constant responsibilities, the freedom from having people depend on you, the freedom from having to go to work every day. It's the freedom to have fun, to be wild and carefree, to hang out, listen to music, and be with friends.

I know, I know—that's not how you see your life. You feel burdens and restrictions, you have people who depend on you, and you have to do a lot of things you'd rather not do. That's all very true, and you won't get any argument from me. But I'm trying to describe how your parents may feel, regardless of whether you think their feelings are justified.

Chances are that your parents' jealousies aren't visible on the surface. Your folks may have them and not even know it. But if jealousies do exist, they're certain to cause problems as unrecognized yet powerful elements in family conflicts.

There are other aspects of your parents' lives and feelings that have an effect on you. I'm sure you're familiar with the old "Mom-must-have-had-a-hard-day-at-the-office" phenomenon. Barely has she stepped into the house and tripped over your skateboard before she launches a full-scale attack in your direction. It's clear to you that she's taking the day's frustrations out on your innocent but convenient persona. Perhaps you can be tolerant. On the other hand, if *you* had a bad day too—uh-oh, look out!

In addition to bad days, parents have a full complement of the worries, pressures, and crises that tend to accompany the living. While they may try to appear strong and secure, while they may want you to think they're gods—while you may even want to think they're gods—they're not. They're human, and that means they're going to worry about jobs, friends, kids, health, money, marriage, and relatives.

You left your school books on the subway; $45 to replace them. The car broke down; $1,500 to fix it. Your coat got stolen; $75 to buy a new one. Your sister needs braces; $2,000. Stock market's down; savings are gone; food stamps are all used up. There have been layoffs at the company; your father's getting an ulcer. Your mom and dad argue more than they used to, the neighbors are griping about the dog, and your grandparents are giving them a hard time (and you know what a hard time parents can give their children!).

Meanwhile, all that conflict with you kids doesn't help any. Your parents feel trapped, overburdened, and caught up in a rat race to stay ahead, pay the bills, and care for the children. No wonder freedom and responsibility become such hot items to them. They see you as having all the freedom and themselves as having all the responsibility. Of course, it's not that simple, but, as you bring them up, you'll need to know how to deal with and respond to these feelings.

## Great Expectations

I have yet to meet parents who don't harbor great expectations for their children, and you're going to have a dickens of a time dealing with them. I'm not talking about the "We expect you to be home at six o'clock" type of expectation, or even the "We expect more from you, young lady" sort of snidery. No, I'm talking about those expectations that have nothing to do with who you are, and everything to do with who your parents want you to be—those expectations that represent Image of Child, *their* Child, *their* Perfect, Idealized Child, *their* Perfect, Idealized, Reflection-of-Parental-Interests-and-Status Child. These expectations are natural, practically unavoidable, and extraordinarily dangerous.

All of us (yes, you, too) hold out images of how we would like people to be—especially people we care about. These images are based upon who we are or aren't, what we were or weren't. Since that tends to cover just about every base, you can begin to see how all-encompassing these expectations are.

If Dad was the big school athlete when he was your age, he may be very disappointed if you're not. If Dad wasn't the big school athlete when he was your age, he may be very disappointed if you are. If he was a total dud in high school, lower on the social ladder than that nerdy nose-picker in math class, he may hope that you become a big social mover. He may push you to date and have girlfriends before you feel ready. He'll want you to have what he always wanted but never had for himself. Of course, if you're popular, he could also resent it; he might feel an old, deep hurt stirring from childhood memories, and unconsciously work to thwart or sabotage your social life.

For many parents, having children is a way of reliving their own childhood. It's a second chance, and they'll wish for you to have the skills and traits that brought them success or pleasure when they were young, or to have the

skills and traits they didn't have but always wanted, or to have the skills and traits they value now. Whew, no wonder expectations are everywhere! They can come at you from the past, the present, and the future.

These expectations have little to do with who you are and a lot to do with who your parents are. That's why expectations can cause so much damage. They're rooted in fantasy rather than reality, and in order to contort you to their Image of Child, your parents must constantly seek to mold, criticize, and notice every time you don't fit the picture. These expectations become the psychological equivalent of trying to force a square peg into a round hole. You're going to get hurt.

Think of all the problems that arise when your looks, speech, interests, friends, clothes, achievements, and values don't meet your parents' vision for you. That's because these expectations are all based on *rejection*. They imply that the way you are isn't good enough.

Expectations based on *acceptance* are quite another kettle of wish. These can be positive, helpful, supportive. They're based on your strengths, a belief in your abilities, confidence in your good judgment and perseverance. They say, "We're behind you, we trust in you, we know you can be the best you want to be." These expectations find the balance between your individuality and your parents' understandable desires for you to be happy, productive, and involved.

These expectations encourage growth and confidence. These expectations are all too infrequently found. But given time, you'll be able to help your parents change their expectations of you from ones of rejection to ones of acceptance. Stay tuned.

## Gimme, Gimme and the Responsibility Gap

Your parents probably feel that you have expectations for them. You expect them to be there, to provide, to buy, to cook, to give up, to spend time, to be consistent. These expectations can cause damage, too, if they ignore who your parents are and what they need as human beings, and if they are based upon roles instead of people.

Your parents feel that you expect them to give and give and give; after all, that's their job as parents. I'm sure you've heard the parents' lament:

> *"Gimme, gimme, gimme, that's all I ever hear around here. I want this, I want that. What do you think I am, a money tree? I'm sick and tired of it. I only have one pair of hands and I don't get any help from you. You're spoiled and selfish and you don't know how lucky you are!"*

Your folks feel put upon, taken for granted, and expected to play a role— the role of idealized, perfect parents. You do place demands on them; it can't be helped. Society doesn't allow you to assume much responsibility at your age. You're forced to be dependent. You resent it and your parents resent it, especially if they feel you take the things they do for granted. You're in something of a double bind. You're placed in a dependent position, then attacked for being dependent.

If society allowed you to drive at age 14, you wouldn't always have to ask your parents to take you places. But it doesn't, so you do. If the buses ran at night, you could take them. But they don't, so you can't. If your parents let you ride your bike across town, you would. But they won't, so you don't. You're either stuck at home or it's "Mom, can you give me a ride..." and "Dad, I need a lift ...."

The same goes for money; between school, sports, lessons, chores, homework, and all the other things you want to do (and your parents want you to do), there isn't that much time left over for a job. And even if you found the time, there aren't many places that will offer a job to a 14-year-old. So you're left with your allowance, money from babysitting or working around the house, and a constant need to ask your parents to cough up some change.

Even though your parents understand that being chauffeur and cook and banker goes with the territory, there will be times when they feel that their needs are squeezed out. This is how it can seem from their point of view:

> *"Dad, I gotta go to dance rehearsal. Can you drive me?"*

Dad just got home from work, having stopped at the supermarket, in the rain, in rush hour.

*"But it's Tuesday. I thought dance was on Wednesday."*

*"It is, but they changed it this week."*

*"Well, I don't know. Your brother has a friend over and I can't leave them alone."*

*"But Dad, I gotta go, and I'm going to be late."*

Your dad feels torn in a million directions. Day in, day out. So does your mom.

*"Mom, I need five dollars for a school trip."*

*"Mom, I need a new pair of sneakers."*

*"Mom, Mrs. Snead says it's your turn to drive to skating."*

*"Mom, I'm gonna die if I have to wear this ratty old thing on Friday. Can I have your charge card and go get a new dress tomorrow after school?"*

*"Mom, I need lunch money."*

*"Mom, I need two dollars for a going-away present for Mr. Brownell."*

*"Mom, can Sally sleep over?"*

*"Mom, I have to bring six quiches to French class tomorrow. Can you help me make them?"*

*"Mom, the ski club is going to Killington this year. It's only two hundred and eighty-five dollars. Can I go? Please? Puh-leeeze? I'll pay half if you'll lend it to me. Okay? Please?"*

*"Mom, what's 'square root' mean?"*

*"Yicch. Why are we having casserole again? We had this last night."*

Poor Mom. She's tired, overworked, and she hasn't bought herself a new dress in two years. Her raise didn't come through because of the wage freeze, her mother wants to know why she doesn't visit more often, and your father

has just invited 12 people to dinner tomorrow night. It seems as if all she hears is...

*"Gimme, gimme, gimme. I need, I have to, I want, you must, can I, will you, why not, please, I gotta, it's not fair."*

Your parents clean, work, drive, shop, worry, fix, provide, solve, try, and strive, but it seems like it's never enough. Just once, for 24 hours, they'd love to disappear. No responsibilities, no kids, no demands, no fights, no tears, no nothing. They're caught in the parent trap and a lot of their own needs aren't being met. They love you kids dearly, but sometimes it gets to be...

TOO MUCH!

Parents like to do things for their kids. They don't like to feel obligated to do things for their kids. They want to feel that their efforts are appreciated (even though they have social, moral, and legal obligations to care for their children). Meanwhile, because kids feel they have no choice about depending on parents (after all, they didn't ask to be born, you know), they have a hard time expressing gratitude for those things they can't or aren't allowed to do for themselves. Another negative cycle gets established. Parents resent "having to" and kids resent "having to have done."

In this vicious cycle, both parents and kids lose out because their feelings are not addressed or accepted. Later on in this book, you'll discover how to work with and defuse feelings like these. For now, though, let's look at a few more characteristics of the parent animal designed to promote conflict in the clan.

The economy is a mess.

Terrorism stalks the world.

Hunger and poverty are on the rise.

Nuclear disaster threatens us all.

Teenage pregnancy is at an
all-time high.

And they worry about
my spelling.

# If You Really Want to Worry about Something...

It is part of the parent role to worry. Parents do this for one of two reasons:

1. They don't remember what they were like as teenagers, or
2. They remember all too well what they were like as teenagers.

Either way, their worrying isn't going to do you or them any good. They'll grow to resent you for causing them so much concern, and you'll grow to resent them for having so little faith. Even though worrying comes from good intentions, it is a useless emotion. It doesn't solve anything, and it sends a message (when parents are the ones doing the worrying) that says to the child, "You're inadequate" and "We don't trust your judgment, strength, or competence." This is why kids react so angrily when parents express their concerns.

*"Be careful," your mother pleads as you walk to the edge of a cliff.*

*"Don't you trust me? What do you think I am? Some dummy who can't stand up without falling over?"*

*"Be careful," your best friend warns you as you walk to the edge of a cliff.*

*Your heart warms from this statement of love and protection.*

A lot of techniques in this book will help you to reduce the limiting effect of your parents' worrying on your life and freedom.

# The Hypocritical Oath

Sometimes it seems like your parents are the biggest phonies alive. It's as if they've taken a vow of hypocrisy. Your father, who smokes two packs of cigarettes a day, nearly killed you for buying some chewing tobacco. Your mother, who has three martinis every evening, grounded you for a month for coming home from a party with alcohol on your breath. Your parents lecture you on telling the truth, then turn around and call in sick to work so they can take the day off. And while you know you shouldn't chew tobacco or drink or lie, it

seems that there are two standards: one for your behavior, and one for theirs. When you call them on it, they're ready and waiting with an answer:

*"It's different. We're older."*

*"Just because I do it doesn't mean it's okay for you to do it."*

*"What's all right for an adult is not all right for a child."*

How can you respect that sort of position? You can't. You're extremely sensitive to the hypocrisy of the world, to the double standards and deceptive manipulations that seem to have become an accepted part of the way so many adults conduct their lives.

> *Your elderly next-door neighbor pays a visit. The first thing your mom says is, "Mrs. Crinkle, can I offer you some fresh-baked cookies?" But when you reach for one, she turns and snarls, "How many times have I told you not to eat between meals?"*

How can your parents be so two-faced? They treat you one way when you're alone and another way when people are watching. You could just throw up at the way your mom turns so sweet and polite when her friends are around and, the second they leave, she's back on the warpath. She treats you in ways she wouldn't dream of acting with her peers. In fact, one day when you were so steamed up your ears were whistling Dixie, you imagined what it might be like if your parents treated their friends the same way they treat you....

> *Bob and Irene, the next-door neighbors, are coming over for dinner. Ding-dong. Your parents rush to the door.*
>
> *"Well, it's about time you got here. You're late. I said come at 6:00 and it's 6:15! Where have you been?"*
>
> *"I, er, we, uh—"*
>
> *"Never mind. Are your feet clean? Irene, where on earth did you get that ridiculous blouse? It makes you look like a tramp. So, how have you been?"*
>
> *"Oh, not bad. Last week we—"*

*"Bob, if you don't stop eating those nuts you're going to spoil your appetite. I swear!"*

*"Anyway, last week we—"*

*"Irene, don't talk with your mouth full. So, how's work?"*

*"Not bad. We have a—"*

*"You know, Irene, unless you apply yourself more and show greater responsibility, I don't think you'll ever get promoted."*

*"Why, I never—"*

*"And I don't think you should see that Charlie Winglop in marketing any more. He's nothing but trouble and I don't want you two spending time together."*

*"How dare—"*

*"Dinner's ready. Do you need to go to the bathroom? Are your hands clean?"*

*"I don't believe—"*

*"Bob, don't smack your lips. Hold your fork correctly. Finish your plate or there'll be no dessert for you."*

If this scene actually happened, Bob and Irene would sooner have dinner on Death Row than come back to your house. It seems unthinkable that your parents would speak like this to their friends. What could be more rude and belittling?

Yet they address you with words like these every day. There isn't a single area of your life that's safe from their searing scrutiny: your friends, your hair, your posture, your handwriting, your taste in clothes, movies, food. Everything you do is evaluated and, before you know it, most of your parents' communications are verbal report cards, with a permanent check mark next to "needs improvement":

*"Stand up straight."*

*"Slow down."*

*"Don't be so careless."*

It's enough to make you want to do the exact opposite, just to show them. If they'd only lay off, you'd probably do half of the things they asked. (Well, maybe a quarter.) But you, a true believer in freedom and democracy, resent being a subject in your parents' (benevolently) despotic court. It's not your parents, specifically, that you rebel against. It's the infringement upon your life, liberty, and pursuit of happiness that they represent.

If only it were 1776! What a great revolutionary you'd make. But, alas, it's not, and you're left to write your own declaration of independence without breaking all diplomatic ties to the mother country. It won't be easy. You can see already what a complicated creature the parent animal is, full of love, advice, concern, hope, and nonsense. And that's only part of the story, for we haven't yet taken a look at the other half of this feud chain—the teenager.

Your turn for the hot seat.

# TEENAGERS: CAN'T LIVE WITH 'EM

I'm hesitant to describe this period of your life, to talk about you, to examine the things going on and how they affect you. I'm hesitant because everyone already acts as if you're public property, some object to be owned, labeled, analyzed, dissected, and manipulated. A slab of meat to be graded, stamped, and approved or rejected according to the standards of others, standards in whose making you had no say.

Who do these people think they are to tell you what to feel, how to think, how to act, as if parenthood were a license to overrule the soul and spirit of another?

*"It's a phase."*

*"It's a stage."*

*"How can you know?"*

*"You're not experienced enough."*

*"When you've lived as long as we have...."*

*"When you have kids of your own...."*

It's as if you're a slide in everyone's microscope. Let's stare and glare and poke and prod. Let's ask what you think so we can tell you you're wrong. Let's ask what you feel and laugh at your song.

*"You're acting like a baby."*

*"You're not really in love."*

*"You shouldn't feel that way."*

*"You're too old."*

*"You're too young."*

Judge, judge, judge. Tell, yell, teach, preach, 24 hours a day. It's as if you're along for the ride on someone else's train; you have no choice about what stops to make and what time to make them.

The school game?  All aboard.  Don't like it?  Too bad: you're not in charge.  Here's how it goes: First, you sit.  All day.  Don't tilt your chair.  Don't squirm, don't tap.

*"But it's boring!"*

What do you mean, it's boring?  What's boring about spending six hours a day being talked to?  What's boring about staring all day long at a blackboard, or a movie screen, or a map, or a chart?  What's boring about memorizing names, places, facts, and dates?  If it's boring, it's because you're not paying attention.

*"It's boring because I AM paying attention."*

*"Settle down.  No talking.  Stay in your seat."*

*"But wait a minute—I'm full of energy, bursting at the seams!"*

*"Not in school you're not.  We decide the rules here, remember?"*

*"But I don't like math."*

*"Don't be silly.  All kids need to take algebra."*

*"Did you?"*

*"Don't change the subject."*

*"But I don't like math, and I'm not going to need it later on."*

*"How do you know what you need?"*

*"Well, if I don't know what I need, how can you know what I need?"*

*"Don't be impertinent.  There are a lot of things that are good for you that you won't like."*

*"Why can't I take things that are good for me that I like, too?"*

*"If you like it, it's probably not good for you."*

Do what we say and you're right.  Don't do what we say and you're wrong.  We'll divide you into 100 little percents.  You're a 98, that's an A...but you, you're just a 79, you're only a C, you're not as good...oh, look, there's a B-plus,

that's better than a C, but still not as good as an A...and you, young man, are unsatisfactory. You need improvement.

Teenagers are treated like lower forms of life. You know—the amoeba, the paramecium, the teenager. We'll grade you, right or wrong, pass or fail. Your worth as a person will be judged on the basis of your school performance. No mistakes allowed.

*"But that's not fair. How can you learn if you can't make mistakes? I didn't just get up one day and start walking, you know. I fell down a few times. And who says you know what's most important to learn? Why is history more important than music? Why is science more important than art? How about peace? Maybe there should be a course on peace, or how to be a parent. I know a few people who could have used a course on that. How about getting along with people? How about building a relationship? Fixing a car? Farming a field, or growing a garden? How about sex?"*

Where on earth did he learn about *that?* We certainly didn't teach him!

*"I think it's more important to be kind and generous than to know French, and I think helping us to understand our feelings and values is more important than knowing when the Battle of Hastings was fought. Why don't they teach those things in school? Why don't they grade us on sense of humor? Honesty? Imagination and creativity? Warmth? Caring for people? Is it because those things aren't important, or is it because they don't fit your little multiple-choice world of A, B, C, or none of the above? You don't like it when I'm a person instead of a number, when I challenge a belief you have, when I hold a mirror up to your life and your world, when I act as if I'm just as good a person as you even though I haven't lived as long."*

Adolescence. The anger with no place to go, the fury that feels like hydrochloric acid eating away at your insides, the injustice, the unfairness, the sense of helplessness, the frustration, the fear, the confusion. And the joy. The boundless thrill of new experiences. First loves, first freedoms. The fullness of friendship, the excitement of accomplishment. Think about it: is there any other time of life so rich, so empty, so limitless, so limited, so fascinating,

so boring, so hopeful, so hopeless, where some days never end and others never come?

Yes, I'm hesitant to describe adolescence, to be another voice telling you how it is. But I want to support your life and your struggles. I want to help you find the courage to discover who you are, even if it's not what *they* want, and to be who you are, even if it's different from what *they* expect. I want to describe the nature of adolescence, in private, with no one listening in, for two reasons:

1. In order to bring up parents, you've got to know where *you* are coming from, how *you* fit into the family picture, what role this time of life will have on *your* thoughts, feelings, actions, and attitudes.

2. I want you to realize, during all those times when you feel dumb or scared or abnormal or hurting, that there's nothing wrong with you (in spite of what somebody else may say); that adolescence is a time of deep and conflicting feelings.

## The Four B's

There are four basic life projects for the teenager. They all relate to and over-lap with one another, and any one of them would be more than enough to keep you busy. But all four at once? No wonder adolescence isn't easy!

These four tasks (known as the four B's, absolutely no relation to the three R's) are:

1. Bodies,
2. Belonging,
3. Becoming, and
4. Breaking Away.

Let's look at Bodies first because they can be so much fun to look at.

## 1. Bodies

Your body (and please forgive me if I'm getting too personal) changes during adolescence from the body of a child to the body of a (young) adult. Every moment of the day, hormones are pumping away, causing physical, psycho-logical, and emotional changes. Everything is growing: your arms, legs,

breasts, hips, penis, muscles, hair, feet, toenails, ear wax, nose hairs. (Pick out those that apply to you.)

These physical changes can make you feel proud and able, but they can also cause stress, confusion, embarrassment, and difficulty. You can feel self-conscious, awkward, mismatched. Shoulders too narrow, rear too big. Too short, too tall, too fat, too thin. It isn't easy to be a new size just when you were getting used to the old one. And adults don't make it any easier.

*"Straighten up."*

*"Don't slouch."*

*"Comb your hair."*

*"Go change."*

In adolescence, you have an awareness of yourself (and others) that is more searching and demanding than ever before. Your own body (and how it compares to others) is in the glare of your spotlight. You're trying on new images, new identities, and you want your body to match. It doesn't matter what others say—you're the one you have to please.

*"Ugh. I can't stand my hair. It's too curly. I wish I had hair like yours."*

*"You can have it. I'd give anything to have your curls instead of this flat mess."*

You stare at the mirror.

*"Blecch. I'll try a part on the other side. Yicch. How about in the middle? Ugh. That's even worse. What if I tape it down? I know, I'll let it dry and then comb it over. Maybe if I don't blow dry it. This'll never work. It's too ugly. I can't go out like this. Maybe if I cut it. Oh, what's the use!"*

And on that rare day when your hair comes out just right, nothing else does. A new pimple sprouts, an old one lingers. Your clothes don't fit. You try on 12 outfits. The black T-shirt? Makes your neck too long. Your favorite pair of jeans? Too short. Sweater? Too floppy. Shorts? Legs too bony. Finally, after the contents of your closet have been re-hung on the floor, you find something that works.

**35**

Uh-oh, not so fast.

*"Where do you think you're going dressed like that?"*

*"But, Mom—"*

*"No buts.  No child of mine is going to school dressed like that.  Hurry up and change or you'll be late."*

*"Mom!"*

*"Now! "*

Naturally, by the time you change and rush off, your hair is no longer right. You can't win.

As if you didn't have enough problems, those hormones causing your body to change so drastically are also at work presenting you with new sexual feelings, desires, and functions.  While you've always been a sexual being, the changes in your physiology and the heightened self-awareness you now possess combine to make sexual thoughts and interests a major force in your life.

Society plays a nasty trick on you as far as teenage sexuality is concerned. It used to be that people died at a much younger age than they do now. Average life spans of 40 or 50 years were the norm.  This tended to speed up the life cycle.  Kids became "adults" at much younger ages, often marrying, having children, and becoming established in a career or a trade in their teens. It worked out quite well.  Sex drives and life roles were synchronized.  Society provided appropriate outlets (in the form of early marriage and "adulthood") for these natural feelings.

Today, however, people can expect to live into their 70s and 80s.  A new life phase—adolescence—has been invented to help fill the time.  Now you've got high school, post-grad years before college, college, a year off to get yourself together, maybe a year abroad, a year to see what work is all about, a couple of years of graduate school, still more years to prepare for a profession. Meanwhile, you've got the world advising you to wait:  Don't get married yet. Don't have kids yet.  Don't get tied down so young.

By the time you add up all these years and admonitions, you've got millions of kids who aren't going to be marrying and having families until their middle to late 20s and beyond, but who are going to be feeling strong, persistent

sexual urges and interests starting in their early teens. Nature and societal roles are now way out of synch with each other. You've got a problem.

Does society help you out? Of course not; it only makes things worse. Society gives you a message so confusing, so hypocritical, so unrealistic, and so insulting that you'd swear it had to come from your parents. But, for once, they're innocent.

It's our culture that bombards you with sexual stimulation. Sex sells, so sex it is. Sex on magazine covers, sex in song lyrics, sex on billboards. Golden bodies in bikini underwear high above Times Square. Want the guys to fall for you? Buy our shampoo. We'll even put it in a bottle that looks like a penis. Want the sexiest girls? Buy our blue jeans. One girl not enough? Use our aftershave and you'll have *two*, not one but *two* girls on each arm. "Do you want to get l-l-l-ucky?" coos the girl in the tight T-shirt. Turn to QSEX on your radio dial or call the 900 number on your TV screen.

Here-a-sex, there-a-sex, everywhere-a-sex-sex. Sex on the silver screen, sex on TV. Hunky dudes who've lost their shirts, beach blondes playing volleyball. Ever wonder why television series are shot in sunny climates? It's so they have an excuse to show beautiful bodies wiggling, squiggling, and giggling their way in front of the camera. In fact, judging from the looks of TV land, three quarters of the world's business is conducted in bathing suits—bedside, poolside, oceanside, or saunaside.

The AIDS crisis only highlights the hypocrisy and immorality of society's stance on teenage and premarital sex. While the media continue to assault kids with sexual stimulation, adults preach abstinence. While teenage television heroes lose their virginity, kids are told to Just Say No to Sex! While the percentage of teenagers and young adults contracting AIDS rises at a rate faster than that of any other segment of the population, adults argue over whether condoms should be made available to teenagers.

Of course, the only safe sex is no sex, and many teenagers are deciding to wait to have sex until they are much older or married. But for those teenagers who are sexually active, the use of condoms significantly reduces the risk of pregnancy and contracting AIDS and other sexually transmitted diseases.

*"With all the dangers of sex, can't we at least have sex education in school? And maybe kids should be able to get condoms in school, too."*

37

*"Condoms in school???!!??? If we handed out condoms, we'd be encouraging sex."*

*"No, you'd be encouraging responsibility."*

*"Kids your age shouldn't be having sex in the first place."*

*"What about sex education, then?"*

*"Sex education in schools? Harummph! No way. Well, maybe. But only in high school."*

*"But some kids have sex before then."*

*"Well, they shouldn't."*

*"But they do."*

*"All right. We'll start sex ed in junior high. But only if your parents approve. And there are certain things you can't talk about."*

*"Like what?"*

*"If I told you, I'd be talking about them."*

*"You mean stuff like abortion and homosexuality?"*

*"You're too young to know about those things."*

All right! So you won't have sex until *they* say you're ready. But wait...what's that other voice you hear?

*"Hey, kid! What's wrong with you? You some sorta of wussy? Eighteen and still a virgin? Gawd, where have you been? Get with it, will ya?"*

Society sends mixed messages; you and your parents get caught in the middle. You're damned if you do and damned if you don't. Meanwhile, your hormones remain unswayed by the double standards and raging controversy.

Now don't get me wrong; I'm not against sex. Some of my best friends have sex. But I am against a hypocritical and greedy society that bathes you in sexual stimulation and then makes believe that you're too young to have sexual feelings and thoughts. I am against a society that's not embarrassed to use sex to make a buck but is too embarrassed to confront teenage sexuality with

honesty and realistic expectations—a society that advertises hemorrhoidal creams and vaginal deodorants on TV but won't accept ads for condoms.

It all adds up to making the life of a teenager even tougher than it already is. Where can you find people with answers? People who know a little more? People not quite as scared and confused by it all as yourself? Where can you turn for support and advice? Why, to your friends, naturally.

## 2. Belonging

If anything terrifies adults more than teenagers, it's their *peers*. Not the holding-up-docks, boats-crashing-into sort of "piers," but the best friends, hanging-out, having fun, getting-into-trouble sort of "peers." Peers as in parties, homework, sleeping over, shopping, laughing, sharing, telling secrets. Peers as in:

> **peer pressure (pēr presh´ər), n.** 1. every parent's nightmare.
> 2. a dreaded disease that strikes down adolescents in their prime. 3. a deadly infection of the mind and body that slowly poisons lovable, kind, and good children who used to do what they were told.

Who are the carriers of this evil, insidious illness? Your friends, of course. Generally, nice folks like you who are also discovering the joys and excitement of teenage time-sharing.

Now I'm not denying (and I hope you're not either) that people do things (or don't do things) because of pressure from others. How about that time you ate 24 donuts because your buddies egged you on, or the time you snuck out of the house in the wee hours to meet your friends? You felt pressure—pressure to belong, to be accepted, to be seen as cool, brave, mature, and adventurous.

But where did that pressure really come from? Was it outside of you, coming from your friends? Or was it inside of you, coming from yourself? Either way, your friends are your partners in exploring life and feelings. They may create certain pressures, but they also relieve some of the pressures you feel. Because of them, you're not alone. You can confide, compare, share, experiment, learn, and love with your friends. Who else are you going to do it with? Your cat?

**39**

Getting along with your own social group—belonging—is an essential project of adolescence. So what else is new? Adults want to belong, too. They act certain ways because of pressures from society, or because the neighbors will be impressed. They are influenced by fads and fears and what the boss will say and the relatives will think. However, when it's adults, they call it "social responsibility" and "sensitivity to the wishes of others." When it's you, they call it "peer pressure."

Whatever it's called, it's another big item on your parents' List Of Things To Worry About. It's also something you worry about. It's hard to find the balance between being your own person and wanting to be accepted and liked. When do you conform so you won't stick out, and when do you strike a blow for individuality? Meanwhile, your parents want to ensure that if anyone's going to influence you, it's going to be them.

The issue of peer pressure may be a large conflict in your household. But it's basically a trust issue. As you take steps to increase your parents' trust in you (something you'll learn in Chapter 2), their fears that you will fall victim to peer pressure should gradually diminish and eventually disappear.

## 3. Becoming

This is a big one, all right. From the day you were born, you've been becoming. And you'll keep on becoming until the day you die.

It's during adolescence that you develop the ability to step outside of yourself and to look at who you are, to think of who you want to become, and to see yourself as others do. You're no longer the little kid who is unaware of appearances and how others respond. Now you have the blessing and burden of a new power of vision.

*Who are you?* What do you care about? What do you want to be? Where are you heading? How are you going to get there? What do you like? What do you hate? Why do you hate? What do you feel? Is it okay to feel that? Where do you hurt? Trying to put it all together so you feel like one person you can know, like, and look after is no piece of double-fudge devil's food cake.

Life can be so confusing. You want to be brave, but you feel scared. You want to do well in school, but you can't stand homework. You want to get along with your parents, but you hate their nagging. You want your friends to like you, but sometimes you do things with them you later regret. Sometimes

it seems as if you're out of control, as if your heart and mind and body are all tearing you apart.

*Who are you?* Are you loyal? Generous? Sexy? Dull? Are you who you think you are? Your parents tell you you're one person and want you to be another. Your boyfriend wants this, your girlfriend wants that. Your teachers expect no less, your parents expect much more. Do this, do that. Be this, be that. One day you're happy, the next you're in tears. You like yourself, you hate yourself. How do you sort it out—the feelings, the tugs, the contradictions?

This is the time when it's all happening—who you are in relation to your parents (Breaking Away) and who you are in relation to your physiology (Bodies) and who you are in relation to your friends (Belonging) and who you are as a human being with feelings, hopes, plans, loves, and hates (Becoming).

Adolescence can be a time of opposites, tensions, extremes. Your best friend today may be your worst enemy tomorrow. One minute you're confident, king of the roost, stepping out, there ain't nothin' you can't do. And the next you're afraid—of yourself, your feelings, your family, your friends, your future. You want to hide, disappear, crawl in a hole and never come out.

But wait a minute. You're back on top of the world—you've met a special friend, your parents have laid off for a while, you've aced a test, you got a fabulous new pair of sneakers. Uh-oh, bombs away, you got cut from the team, had a fight with a friend, the teacher you liked made a fool of you in class. You're flunking science, your parents have grounded you, and it's no allowance for three weeks. Wait a sec, you hop out of bed, who is that gorgeous face in the mirror, what a bod, who is that, why, it's you—on track, in charge. Look out, world!

> *"I wish I were dead. I can't stand it anymore. I hate myself. Nobody likes me. I'm stupid and ugly and it'll never change. Oh, God, I wish I were dead. Then they'd be sorry."*

You lie in bed, stare at the ceiling, count the dead flies in the light fixture. All's a blur—eyes out of focus, nose out of joint. You're up, down, in, out, good, bad, happy, sad, in the clouds, underground. Will it ever end?

*There's nothing wrong with you.* Adolescence can be hard. So much of what you're experiencing is new and different. Everything's changing, and while change is exciting, valuable, and unavoidable, it's still scary. It rocks your boat. You're constantly tested, challenged, and set up in a world that only

**41**

seems to recognize success or failure. You have more opportunities than ever before, yet there are also more limits, expectations, and pressures. You don't have a long track record of experience to give you comfort. You can't say, "I've been there before. I know I'll get through this. I know I'll do okay."

What you need is a strong, secure identity, a reassuring sense of who you are and what you can do. If you had that, you could sail through adolescence—no sweat. There's just one problem. Adolescence is the time when you're building that sense of identity, purpose, and confidence. Adolescence is the struggle. The very skills and experiences you need to cope with adolescence are the very ones you don't yet have and won't have until you're much older.

Meanwhile, it doesn't help to have everyone else focusing on what you did wrong, what didn't work, how you blew it, where you messed up. You don't need people to monitor your failures with the smug radar of experience. You know when things go wrong. What you could use is someone to tell you when things go right.

What you've got to do is hang in there and focus on your journey instead of your goal. Everyone else will watch your goals for you. Let them. Let them worry about whether your train is on schedule, making all the right stops, pulling in to the right stations. Let them worry while you look out the window and enjoy the ride.

Use that spotlight outside yourself to illuminate this incredible time of your life. When the bottom of your life has fallen clear through to China, cry, scream, moan, and stomp. Then congratulate yourself and feel good that you're capable of deep emotion and expression. Be glad that you're not one of those uh-duh morons who coast through life on a cushion of bland and benign. You're a full-blasted live wire who's going to soar higher than your dreams and farther than your limits. But with the highs come the lows, the valleys, the subterranean tombs of disappointment and dark despair.

Be sad, be angry, be upset, be impatient, accept yourself, accept your feelings, make the changes you want—dive in and take control of your life—even when it seems most out of control. Get used to it now. A day will come when there aren't parents, or teachers, or friends telling you how to be, and when it does, won't you be glad you know who you are?

## 4. Breaking Away

If you're sitting there saying, "Holy tofu, no wonder life can get so tough with so much happening," hold on a minute, 'cause we're not finished. There's more.

Adolescence is also the time when you begin to break away from your parents. This is healthy, necessary, and painfully difficult, for you and for them. For most of your life, you've been completely dependent on your parents. Hopefully, they fed you, clothed you, cared for you, and kissed it to make it better. They rocked you, burped you, and wiped your wet little behind. They were your passport to the world. They took you to the park, the zoo, the shopping plaza. They chose your toys, your books, and even your friends. Just about everything you wanted had to pass through the gates of parental permission. They controlled your life, your limits, your behavior.

When you're two or five or eight years old, that's not such a bad deal. But now you're much more your own person. You've developed your own interests, values, and priorities. You want (and should have) more control over your own life. You want to choose your own friends, clothes, and music; you want to make your own decisions and mistakes. You want more freedom, more privileges, more respect. You're less willing to accept your parents' "because-I-said-so" authority.

Meanwhile, your parents are used to telling you what to do and when to do it. They're not used to your saying, "No, I won't," and "You can't make me." What makes this all so difficult is that you can't (yet) be totally independent of your parents. You still need them for food, shelter, money, protection, and emotional support. You still find it handy to be able to blame things on your folks: "I'd do it, but my parents won't let me." So while you have to remain dependent to a degree, you're struggling for more and more independence.

This creates tension and resentment. You resent your parents for still having control, and they resent you for being so ungrateful. You're both acting out valid feelings in response to your age and position in the family.

*"As long as we pay the bills, you'll do what we say."*

*"As long as you live in this house, you'll follow our rules."*

But you can't help living in their house at age 15, and you don't like the fact that this unavoidable twist of fate cuts into what you see as your inalienable right to freedom of choice. Meanwhile, your parents feel that because they're supporting you and are still responsible for you, it gives them major say-so in what you do. There's logic to both points of view, but obviously they work against each other.

Somehow a compromise has to be reached so that your rights, needs, and individuality can be respected and, at the same time, your parents don't feel suckered into supporting a lifestyle or set of values they can't stomach. It's easy to find this balance when positions are extreme. You'd agree that your parents aren't obligated to let you sell drugs, have wild orgies, or make counterfeit money under their roof. But it gets much, much trickier when your behavior isn't extreme, when the conflicts are ones of style, taste, fashion, attitude, interests, and priorities.

What you need are ways to reach a happy middle ground. Here you are, trying to come to terms with life, love, liberty, and leave-taking, and your parents seem only to make things harder than they already are. Some days it seems like two steps forward and 83 steps back. No wonder you feel pressured, tense, impatient, and moody. It's enough to make anyone want to grow up in a hurry!

It's enough to make your parents want you to grow up in a hurry, for your adolescence can be hard on them, too. What would they say if someone asked them to describe teenage children? What would their complaints be on a day when they're feeling unloved and underappreciated?

*"Teenagers can be so cruel and self-centered."*

*"They act like such know-it-alls."*

*"You can't tell them anything."*

*"My kid's so moody and emotional I never know what to expect."*

*"My daughter behaves as if I don't even exist."*

*"They only think of themselves."*

*"They never talk to me unless they want something or have a complaint."*

From a parent's point of view, this is how teenagers can come across. It figures. If you're experiencing tons of new feelings and situations, you can be moody and overreactive. You can take things too seriously. If your confidence is constantly under attack, you can compensate by showing off, by being a know-it-all. If you're struggling to cut ties to your folks, you can be cruel and rejecting.

If you're under pressure and preoccupied with problems, you can act like your parents don't exist, then tune back in to them when you want something. It's maddening to your parents when you reject their advice. Experience does count. You know you're wiser now than when you were four, and that your judgment, intellect, and emotional control will be sharper still in another ten years' time. There are occasions when your parents' experience does provide greater insight than yours. No wonder they get frustrated! Yet it's equally

frustrating to be told what to do by someone else. It's reasonable that you would want to live and make decisions based on your experience.

Just as the things your parents do that bother you can be explained by their feelings of love and concern, the things you do that bother them can be explained by the nature of adolescence. Of course, explanations can't lessen the pain of colliding roles. This is why the conflicts between parents and teenagers are so tricky: You're *both* right. You have every right to feel the way you do, and they have every right to feel the way they do.

Unfortunately, each role damages the other. The needs of parents and the needs of teenagers are at odds with one another. If you can get out of your roles and begin to relate as people, if you can say you're both right and take it from there, you'll stand the best chance of liking each other and, most importantly, liking yourselves. And people who like themselves are remarkably easier to get along with.

# Chapter 2

# GETTING DOWN TO BASICS:

## ISSUES AT THE CORE OF EVERY PARENT-CHILD RELATIONSHIP

*Whether you're super punk or totally preppie, new wave or old money, valley girl or country boy, ultra chic or extra meek....*

*Whether you're up the creek or down the tubes, close to the edge or far from the madding crowd....*

*If you want to bring up parents who'll stay off your back, who'll trust you, who'll give you more freedom and greater responsibilities....*

*Then you'll need to master these basics of every parent-teenager relationship.*

GETTING
DOWN TO
BASICS

# INTELLIGENCE-GATHERING

You may take one look at your parents and say, "Well, there's certainly not much intelligence gathered here." Perhaps. It doesn't mean that you can skip this chapter, though. Whether your parents' cup of intelligence runneth over or leaketh out isn't the point.

The point is that in order to bring up parents, you have to first understand and accept them where they are. While you are to be forgiven for dreaming of a mother and father who lavish praise, respect, and $20 bills on you, when you come back down to earth you'll find, for better or worse, the same old folks at home. Before you can move them along in directions more to your choosing, you must know who they are and what makes them tick. That means finding out as much about them as you can.

49

How?

By asking questions. And then listening—carefully—to what they have to say. For tucked away in your parents' somniferous soliloquies are valuable nuggets of information you can use to solve problems and smooth relationships. And if the thought of actually talking with your parents makes you weak in the knees, don't think of it as talking, think of it as panning for gold!

Why does intelligence-gathering work?

1. Because the data you dig up will suggest issues and attitudes underlying present problems.

2. Because your parents will be pleased that you care enough to ask, and that you show interest in them.

3. Because time spent talking is time spent not fighting. That right there will cut down on conflict.

People, and I suppose we can safely include your parents in that broad category, are made of much more than sugar and spice and the not-so-infrequent vice. Your parents' behavior and attitudes towards you are the result of their:

- childhood experiences,
- relationships with their parents,
- social histories,
- health,
- personalities,
- fears and insecurities,
- hopes and expectations,
- careers,
- marriage (or marriages),
- other relationships and friendships,
- experiences with your brothers and sisters, and
- current emotional status.

In other words, *who your parents are*—that combination of experience and personality that has shaped their lives so far—is going to affect *you*. How can you expect to help them mature, to anticipate their attitudes, predict their reactions, avoid their sensitive spots, and know how to talk to them if you

don't gather as much intelligence as you can about their lives, experiences, and feelings?

In the area of foreign policy, our government constantly seeks to discover everything it can about leaders of other nations. This information is essential in planning negotiations and assessing the risks involved in various strategies. Given how foreign some of your parents' policies must seem, it should be no different in your own homeland.

Be forewarned that I'm going to focus solely on moral methods of intelligence-gathering. I'll leave the less-than-moral methods to your ingenuity and conscience. I can't condone, nor do I need to teach, those strategies that rely upon subterfuge, deception, invasion of privacy, or breaking and entering. If you choose to keep yourself informed via eavesdropping, rifling through drawers, and sneaking peeks into wallets or purses, even for purposes so lofty as discovering your birthday presents or your parents' sex books, it'll have to be on your account, not mine.

The methods I support are those that:

- increase your parents' good feelings towards you and about themselves, and
- provide valuable information for the purposes of planning how to get what you want and need.

That's the great thing about moral intelligence-gathering—you can kill two birds with one stone. You get valuable information and, in the process, your parents feel flattered and touched by your interest (which comes around again to improve your standing).

So, are you ready to gather some intelligence?

Then take your mark, get set—

**Hold it!!!**

Before you assault and pepper your parents with questions, here are a few tips you need to know:

- Start with simple, non-threatening, not-too-personal questions:

*"How was your trip?"*

*"What did you think of the movie?"*

*"Did the meeting go all right?"*

Depending on how your parents respond, slowly move into other, more personal areas:

*"Are you under a lot of pressure at work?"*

*"Did that phone call from Uncle Hal upset you?"*

*"What did you dream about doing when you were a kid?"*

■ Be careful how you phrase your questions. You don't want to put your parents on the defensive. Choose words that aren't likely to hurt or upset them. For example:

| Bad Style | Good Style |
|---|---|
| *"Dad, were you always such a jerk or is it something you learned as an adult?"* | *"Dad, what were you like when you were a kid? Do you think you changed a lot when you grew up?"* |
| *"Mom, how come you're in such a bad mood and picking on me?"* | *"Mom, am I doing anything that's making you angry?"* |
| *"Were your parents as mean to you as you are to me?"* | *"What kind of discipline did your parents use with you and your sister?"* |

Style is so important that I'm going to go into it in greater detail later in this chapter. But I thought an early warning was necessary for those of you who ask questions first and shoot later. (Actually, forget the shooting. Stick with the questions.)

So, are you ready?

Then take your mark, get set —

*"Hold it!"*

What's the matter?

*"This'll never work. You don't know my parents. They don't tell me anything. They just say, 'Mind your own business.' If I ask, 'How was work?' they say, 'Okay.' If I ask, 'What'd you do?' they say, 'Nothin.'"*

I see the problem. In other words, what do you do if your parents don't want to talk about themselves?

*"Exactly."*

And what do you do if your parents resent being questioned?

*"Precisely."*

And what do you do if they feel attacked and invaded and defensive?

*"Decidedly so."*

In other words, what do you do if they act just like you?

*"No!!! Well, er, maybe, er, maybe I'm a little like that...but I'm trying to change."*

Good for you! And if you're trying to change, you know how difficult that can be. So what you're going to have to do is help your parents to feel at ease with this new, more intimate pattern of communication.

*"How?"*

■ Model the response you'd like to see in your parents. Be open to *their* questions. Don't get defensive. Don't assume there's an implied criticism in everything they ask.

■ If you feel that something is "none of their business," say so—but say it like this:

*"I wouldn't feel comfortable talking about that."*

*"That's kind of private. I think I'd like to keep it to myself."*

■ Be patient. Don't push. Let your parents work up to increased levels of trust and revelation at their own speed.

■ Don't jump on, judge, or criticize your parents' responses.

■ Avoid inflammatory issues. Notice which topics your parents are most comfortable with and build upon those.

■ Be flexible. If one method doesn't work (such as asking questions over dinner), try another. For example:

*"Dad, how'd you like to spend some Peripatetic time together?"*

You'll have to explain to your dad, unless he studied Greek history in kinder-garten, that this means taking a walk—as followers of Aristotle did in the ancient Lyceum of Athens—for purposes of instruction and enlightenment.

- Gather intelligence about your parents from other sources:  relatives, family friends, brothers and sisters.  You'll not only get the facts about the folks, but you'll learn things that will help you to approach them directly.
- Read the rest of this chapter carefully.  Pay particular attention to the pointers it gives about timing, style, and respecting your parents' privacy.

With these introductory tips out of the way, now are you ready to plumb your parents' lives and reap the fruits of intelligence-gathering?  Are you ready to become the apple of your parents' eyes?  Are you ready to use these peachy techniques as the kiwis to better communication, kumquat may?

Then take your mark, get set —

*"Hold it!!!!"*

What is it *now?*

*"What do I do if my parents get all suspicious and say, 'Why are you asking so many questions?'"*

Tell them:

*"Mom, Dad, in a world as fractured and stressful as ours—with crumbling schools, economies, and infrastructures; with people feeling disconnected spiritually, emotionally, and socially; with government, religion, and family values under attack from the right and the left; with crime, drugs, and AIDS laying siege to whole nations— I just thought it might be a good idea to strengthen our family ties a little bit."*

# It's 1967. Do You Know Where Your Parents Are?

You must discover everything you can about your parents' childhood and adolescent years. Don't wait until you get caught by the old "when-I-was-your-age" routine. Those reminiscences are generally colored by the point your parents are trying to make in the present. Since so many of their current feelings and decisions about you will connect with their early lives, the past is the place to start.

- Where did they grow up? A big city? A small town? In the country? Overseas?

- Who did they grow up with? Parents? Step-parents? Guardians? Brothers? Sisters? Pets? Was either one an only child? Was either one adopted?

- Were they poor? Rich? In-between? What did their parents do? What did money mean to the family?

- How about school? Did they like it? Hate it? Did they do well? Did they get into trouble? What kinds of parties did they go to? How did they deal with drugs or drinking?

- Did they have friends? Did they date? Did they have sex? Did they worry about sex? Feel pressured? How did their parents deal with issues of sex? (You'll have to judge if your parents are mature enough to discuss this topic.)

- What did your folks do to have fun as kids? Were they popular? Did they get along with their siblings? What did they fight about with their parents? With their friends?

- When did they get their first jobs? When did they leave home for the first time? How much freedom did they have when they were still living at home?

- What were the cultural forces and values at the time they grew up? Was there a war? A bad economy? A boom period? An explosive new technological discovery? (You know, like the wheel or something.)

- How did your parents meet? What was their courtship like? Who popped the will-you-marry-me question? What was the wedding like? Has their marriage turned out the way they expected?

- And, most important of all, how did they feel as kids? Did they like themselves? Were they happy most of the time? Worried? Afraid? Angry? Sad? Devil-may-care? How did they feel about their families, friends, schooling? How did they feel in those situations you're experiencing now?

Naturally, you can't find all of this out overnight. It will take time, but you'll be amply rewarded for your efforts. The intelligence you gather will explain a lot of your parents' present values and attitudes. You'll be able to figure out when and if there are hidden issues at work beneath a current conflict, and what they are. For example, if your parents were poor as kids but have some money now, this may affect how they react to your attitudes towards money, just as your childhood experiences with money will form part of your adult perspective. If they led unusually sheltered lives as kids, that could explain why they restrict you so much, or even why they let you run wild.

Search for connections between the problems you're having with your parents and their own adolescent experiences. That's where you'll find clues to the real nature of a conflict. Are your folks giving you a hard time because of the way you fight with your siblings? Find out about your parents' sibling relationships. This information may illuminate the issue.

How about your room? Too messy for Mom and Dad? Maybe it *is* a disaster area, but maybe there's a hidden agenda loose (see Chapter 5). Perhaps they never had a room of their own when they were kids, and it bothers them that you keep the room they always wanted looking like a war zone. See? You grew up thinking it's natural to have a room of your own. They never had one, so it's only logical that you value private space in different ways.

Did they have to work after school as kids to help support the family? Maybe they vowed that no kid of theirs would ever have to do the same thing. On the other hand, the experience could have been so beneficial that they want you kids to work, even though you don't have to.

Did your mother's sister drown as a child? Maybe that's why your mom is so bossy when you're at the beach. Was your father's father an alcoholic? No wonder your dad is so strict about drinking. Did your mom have an abortion during college? That could explain why she's so concerned now that you're beginning to date. Did your dad drop out of school when he was 16? That's bound to have an impact on how he might react to your desire to do the same. Did your mom love going away to Camp Mosquito when she was a girl? Maybe that's why she wants to send you there this summer. Did your dad get a lot of enjoyment from music lessons as a kid? Maybe that's why...well, you get the picture.

It's funny how parents incorporate their childhood experiences into raising their own kids. They seem to either repeat the patterns—to relate to their kids as their parents related to them—or to do the opposite in reaction to their own upbringing. Parents also tend to assume that their experiences were universal, that what worked for them should work for their kids. Of course, this position overlooks two important factors:

1. The culture and times in which they grew up are different from those in which you are growing up, and

2. You're a completely different individual from your parents.

While experience is valuable, and there is insight your parents can offer, it's crucial that both you and your parents recognize that you are different people, with different interests, priorities, and cultural backgrounds. When dealing with conflict, it's essential to be able to separate your feelings and their feelings, your personality and theirs, your society and theirs. Too often, parents and kids have problems because they approach an issue with totally different, yet equally valid, associations and assumptions. This must be acknowledged.

As you learn more about your parents, you'll identify the sources of their present-day concerns and decisions. You'll trace their attitudes to various people, places, and experiences that influenced them. This will be helpful for two reasons:

1. A previously troubling position of theirs may suddenly become acceptable once you realize where they're coming from, and

2. The knowledge you gain may be useful in devising tactics for approaching a tricky problem.

By combining the intelligence you gather with the communications skills presented in this book, you'll help your parents to see when and how they're laying their own values and experiences on you. Of course, laying values on you is not automatically bad. After all, wouldn't you want your parents to bring you up according to values that embrace honesty, generosity, kindness, creativity, humor, and *joie de vivre*? (Look it up!) The trouble starts when values, tastes, and changing times overlap and become confused, when the standards that were perfectly appropriate to one generation are applied to another in ways that no longer make sense.

As you scurry merrily about, filling your basket with the flowers of your parents' lives, keep in mind the importance of *style*. You have to be very careful when gathering intelligence that you don't judge your parents' feelings and experiences. You know how much you hate it when they judge your feelings and opinions, when they put a "right" or "wrong" or "silly" or "dumb" label on things you feel and say. It just wouldn't be fair, and it wouldn't set the right example for them to follow, if you solicited information and then turned it around to use as an attack.

*"Say, Dad, when you were in junior high, did you date a lot?
I mean, like, were you popular, did you have lots of girlfriends?"*

*"As a matter of fact, son, I didn't know what a girl was. I had no friends and didn't go on a date until college."*

*"Ah ha! I knew it! Just 'cause you were a social wipeout weirdo is why you won't let me go out. I bet you're jealous."*

Uh-uh. No fair. This style won't win you any friends or influence. Tread gently. A much better follow-up line would be:

*"Gosh, how'd that make you feel, Dad?"*

Further sympathetic listening would give Dad the support he may have never received for his childhood ache. Once he sensed that his feelings were understood and accepted, you could say:

*"You know, Dad, hearing about your childhood, I wonder what effect it has on how you feel about my dating and spending so much time with friends."*

Much better.
Much worse:

*"Mom, how was it that your brother died when you were my age?"*

*"He was out with some friends and they had been drinking. There was an accident and all five teenagers in the car were killed."*

*"Oh, I get it. Just 'cause your brother was so dumb is why you won't let me ride with friends. You're just taking it out on me."*

Eee-y-ouch!!!! No, no, no! The idea isn't to give you ammunition, it's to give you understanding. You can then take that understanding and carefully, cleverly, use it to encourage your parents to see the role their past plays in your life. If you're probing in sensitive areas, you can't just bludgeon your way in like Attila the Hun with a chip on his shoulder.

Take a second look at this last mother-daughter conversation. What might have happened if the daughter had listened supportively and then said:

*"You must have been crushed."*

*"How did your parents feel?"*

*"Did your parents treat you differently after your brother died?"*

*"How long did you cry?"*

*"I bet you worry that the same thing could happen to me."*

Can't you just feel the difference between those two types of responses? The second version is bound to lead in positive directions, to closeness, sharing, understanding, and perhaps revelation. The mother may see for the first time that she is carrying her grief and fear from this childhood tragedy into her relationship with the daughter.

Choose a style of talking and listening that reflects your respect for the feelings, information, and confidences your parents are sharing. One aspect of style is timing. Choose a good moment for intelligence-gathering. There's no point in getting into a conversation if someone's upset, rushed, preoccupied, or otherwise unavailable to your warm queries. And make sure you leave time to listen. It just wouldn't do to hit an unsuspecting parent with, "What did you think about God and religion when you were a kid?" and announce two minutes later, "Sorry, gotta go watch TV."

Similarly, don't search for intelligence in the midst of a conflict. First, you won't find much, and second, with emotions running high, any questions you ask would seem suspiciously self-serving if not downright antagonistic. You might consider establishing a ritualized time for intelligence-gathering. Perhaps your mom drives you to school every day, and it takes 20 minutes. That's a good opportunity for picking her brain. For one thing, you've got a guaranteed out ("love to talk more, but I gotta go"), and your mother will bask all day in the glowing memory of her early morning intimacies with you. Another good time is when you're home from school sick and there's a parent handy.

Whether you probe your parents' past with methodical calculation or spontaneous curiosity, intelligence-gathering will do wonders.

# Higher Intelligence-Gathering

There are several specialized forms of intelligence work you would be well-advised to master.

In the same way that your parents' experiences while growing up influence their present feelings and attitudes, so do their lives today, as well as the expectations they hold for the future. If three weeks from now they're going

to have to say "yes" or "no," "you can" or "you can't" to some request of yours, you need to know as much as possible about the feelings and forces that will be at work when they make their decision.

Set your sights on discovering how things are going in their lives right now. How do they feel? How's their health? How are their jobs? Any money pressures? Are they being hassled by relatives? Bugged by the IRS? Are your mom and dad getting along? Are they happy and hopeful? Depressed? Did a new contract come through? A promotion? A raise? Has a friend of theirs just died? Are they worried about one of your brothers or sisters?

Find out. Ask questions and show that you care about the answers by using Active Listening techniques. (You'll learn more about these in Chapter 4.) Your parents may have off-limits areas, just as you do, so probe gently. Don't be an uncouth sleuth. If you think you're on shaky ground, you can always preface your remarks with:

*"I'm not sure if it's okay to ask, but...."*

*"It may not be any of my business...."*

*"I wondered if you'd be comfortable talking about...."*

They can only be impressed by your sensitivity to their feelings and privacy. Show them that you take notice of their moods:

*"Gee, Dad, you really seem down today. Something bad happen?"*

*"What's up? You look like you won the lottery!"*

*"Crummy day at work?"*

*"Are you feeling okay?"*

Your sensitivity to your parents' feelings will encourage them to be more accepting of yours.

Another idea to keep in mind is that there are times when you may want to...

## Ask the Other Parent

A good technique. If you have two parents, that means you've got two childhoods to cover. You may want to ask them questions separately; they might talk more freely if it's just one of them and you at a time. It'll be interesting

to compare notes on their experiences. You may discover some good reasons for any conflicts they have with each other, or why your dad is strict about some things and your mom about others. This information can help you decide which parent to go to for what request.

There may be times when you feel uncomfortable bringing up a topic with one of your parents. Then ask the other. Maybe you'd rather ask your mom about your dad's relationship with his parents when he was young. Or ask your dad why Mom seems so nervous and irritable lately. Keep in mind that your questions or conversation may be relayed to the parent you didn't ask. (You know how parents are.) You could request a promise of confidentiality (only you can judge if it will be honored). Or you could use to your advantage the fact that your question will be passed on.

For example, your dad may tell your mom that you asked him why she seemed so nervous. (This could be great for Dad, since it gives him a way to find out himself.) Chances are that your mom will be pleased that you were concerned. It could also prompt her to change her behavior. She may not have realized that she was coming across like a skittish jitterbug.

Remember, though, style is everything. You're not asking your dad,

> **"Why is Mom being such a pain?"**

You're asking,

> **"Do you know if something is upsetting Mom? She seems irritable lately."**

Got that? Right?

## Ask Grandma

Or Grandpa or Uncle Dick or Cousin Bob or Aunt Mary Lou. Relatives (or, lacking relatives, old family friends) can be great sources for the lowdown on your parents' high jinks as youngsters. For one thing, since they don't have to be responsible for you, they will be on your side. This tends to ensure more accurate information. Grandma will have no trouble remembering when your father burned down the garage. Dad may have a foggier recollection of such a trivial event.

Respect your parents' right to present-day privacy. They probably don't want their parents to know any more about their lives than you want your parents to know about yours. Seems fair enough.

As a sleuth in search of truth, don't overlook...

# The Sibling Source Book

Those alternately indispensable and eminently eliminatable creatures known as your brothers and sisters are excellent sources for hot tips and cool logic when it comes to your parents. Don't forget to check their data banks. They may have picked up some valuable nuggets along the way—especially if they're older than you. Leave no stone unturned in your intelligence-gathering mission.

# Assumption Presumption

Let's say you're upset with your parents about something. You make assumptions about why they arrived at a certain decision or position. Based on those assumptions, you prepare to do battle with them.

But how do you know your assumptions are right? Aren't your folks always assuming things about you that aren't true? What if your assumptions are wrong?

Look before you leap. Try to find out what's really going on. You'll avoid putting your foot in your mouth, and you may discover that you have a different reaction once you know your parents' true motivations.

*Your father constantly yells at you these days. You assume he's on your case unfairly, and you're ready to take the bait and snap back. But first, you decide to ask your mom about it. You learn that he just had his annual physical and was told he had a small tumor. Until the results of more testing come back, he won't know if it's serious or nothing to worry about. He didn't mention it because he didn't want you to worry, but the tension he's feeling is coming out anyway.*

Now that you know the strain he's under, aren't you more willing to be tolerant of his yelling? To not hook in or take it personally? To ignore it? Of course you are, now that you know what's behind it.

How about this one?

> *You kids have been asking for a dog for years. Every time the sub-ject comes up, your mom says no. Too messy, too expensive, it'll ruin the furniture. This time, though, you guys have had enough. Your bite is going to be worse than your bark, and you're ready to sink your bicuspids into this issue. Just when you're about to call a bow-wow pow-wow to protest this cruelty to children, your dad takes you aside and explains that your mom was attacked and badly bitten by a dog when she was young. That's why she doesn't want a dog in the house.*

So why didn't she just come out and tell you herself? Good question. The problem is, people don't always act in the most logical or direct fashion. They deny feelings, they distort feelings, they unconsciously convince them-selves of all sorts of things that aren't true, and they disavow all sorts of things that are. Your mom may genuinely be unaware that her childhood trauma is at the core of her refusal to allow a dog. She may really believe that it's the carpeting and the cost of dog food. She may be embarrassed to reveal her fear, and she may be concerned that you kids might develop your own fears from her unfortunate episode.

Whatever the reason, it's important to find it out. There's a big difference between her saying, "Look, I'm terrified, I can't help it, it's too late for me to change," and, "You can't have a dog because I don't think you'll take good care of it." Depending on your understanding of the situation, you're going to have totally different reactions. So why not try to discover the way things really are? Why not check out the accuracy of your assumptions?

There's much to your life that your parents don't know about. As various issues arise, your folks will make their own assumptions about your feelings, attitudes, and motivations. Since they can't be aware of all your inner thoughts, their assumptions may be wrong. They won't always realize the

experiences you've had that influence your actions and values. There could be at least three reasons for this:

1. They may not be very observant,
2. You may keep your life as secret as you can, and/or
3. You may not know all the forces and feelings at work within you.

So give yourself and your parents a break. That's what intelligence-gathering is all about: finding out, checking assumptions, knowing your parents as people. Then take the new information you have and combine it with appropriate style, communication techniques, and behavior strategies. You'll be able to bring up parents who are more in touch with the role their own experiences play in how they treat you. You'll also eliminate all those arguments that come up because somebody made a faulty assumption. Powerful stuff!

# EVERY KID NEEDS A TRUST FUND

Of course. How else can you have the freedom to go places, do things? How else can you feel independent, valued, and respected? How else are you going to get the love and support of your friends and family? Trust funds are essential to successful relationships, to happiness, to getting what you want out of life.

For those of you who ask God to bless Mommy, Daddy, and your margin account at the stockbrocker's in your bedtime prayers, I should point out that I'm not talking about the oodles-of-money-in-it type of trust fund. I'm talking about a much more valuable kind of trust fund. The kind that isn't affected by inflation and greedy relatives. I'm talking about the Real Thing, the "of-course-you-can-dear, we-trust-you" kind of trust fund, the "how-can-we-let-you-drive-a-car, we-can't-even-trust-you-to-ride-your-bike-safely" type of trust fund.

"Oh, *that* kind," you say, the lightbulb of awareness going off over your head. Exactly. That kind, the valuable kind, the irreplaceable kind. The kind that, when you blow it, leads to parental proclamations like:

**"We're so disappointed in you. We trusted you and you let us down."**

**65**

*"I guess we were wrong to trust you."*

Daggers to the heart.

*"How could you be so dumb?  How can we ever trust you again?"*

Lethal guilt.

There's no way you can avoid dealing with trust issues in your family. You have to trust your parents, and they have to trust you.  Sometimes, though, problems with your parents will threaten to undermine the trust that's been built up over the years.  Many of the strategies in this book are designed to keep trust strong, even in the face of conflict.  Disagreement doesn't have to lead to a breakdown in trust if the problem is handled with respect for everyone's needs and feelings.  Since trust is at the core of human relationships, we'd better find out all we can about this powerful force.

Trust is like a bridge. It is, ideally, a strong, durable connection between two places, two people; a conduit that allows the two-way flow of good feeling, intimacy, sharing, and belief.  Trust is an extension of faith in another person's judgment, motivation, and sensitivity.  It allows relationships to grow and deepen and bring increased pleasure.

Every now and then (which, for parents and teenagers, means quite often), something comes along and threatens the trust bridge.

*Your father said he'd take you to the game on Saturday. Saturday rolls around, and Dad goes off to play tennis.*

*"Dad, you said you'd take me to the game."*

*"Oh, my goodness, I completely forgot. I made a date to play tennis with the Tylers. It totally slipped my mind. I'm really sorry. Let's do it next week, I promise."*

Well, you're not exactly jumping for joy. You feel let down. You looked forward to going. How could he forget? If he really wanted to go, he would have remembered. He must not care.

It's easy to feel hurt, duped, and foolish when someone betrays your trust. You went on the line, you took a risk, you said, "I trust you," and look what happened! No wonder you're angry. But nobody's perfect, and chances are you trust your father enough to see his forgetfulness as an honest, unintentional mistake. Off you go to the game next weekend and all is well again.

All is well because you have a basic trust in your father. The bridge is strong and can withstand the occasional ramming of one of its supports. It's a good thing, too, because people are going to mess up from time to time— forget a commitment, hurt a feeling, let a secret slip. As long as the trust bridge is well-established, the structure will hold, even if it's damaged. You'll need to make some fast repairs, however, and you'll need to be extra careful that no further harm occurs. Your bridge is more vulnerable with shaky piers.

The real trouble comes when the bond of trust is so weakened and abused that the whole structure simply collapses. You can't make repairs, you can't continue the flow, there's nothing left at all. Trust has been destroyed, smashed, shattered, blown to smithereens by veritable battleships of betrayal.

You know how that can feel. Your parents hide things from you and embarrass you in front of friends. They ask you to confide in them, then turn around and laugh at your feelings. They belittle your ideas and seem to break promises as fast as they make them. The bike they promised you could get is now being held hostage for improving your grades. The slumber party they swore you could have is now off because they're going out that night.

There's no way you can like and respect your parents if you can't trust them. And since trust is a two-way street—er, bridge—there's no way you can enjoy the privileges and freedom you desire unless your parents trust you.

How does the parent animal look at trust? Trust is a concept parents worship. All rise. All kneel. In Trust is our God. It's a magic word, a state of nirvana. If you can only reach the exalted land of your parents' trust, the world will open up for you like the Red Sea to create a path strewn with promise and privilege.

What does it mean when your parents say they trust you? The question is, trust you to do what? The answers are:

- To be careful. (According to whose standards?)
- To use good judgment. (Based on whose values?)
- To be honest. (What if it hurts someone's feelings?)
- To keep promises. (What if circumstances change?)
- To do what they say. (What if it's wrong?)
- To do what's right. (In whose opinion?)
- To do what's moral. (In whose eyes?)

You can see how easy it is to get into murky territory here. Trust is not always an absolute—yet parents act as if it is. They say, "We can't trust you," when what they really mean is, "You didn't handle the situation the way we would have wanted." Is it that they can't trust *you*, or that they can't trust you to make decisions and take actions consistent with *their* values?

I'm not bringing this up to provide you with a handy excuse. Naturally, kids deserve to lose their parents' trust when they act like selfish, sneaky, suspicious, self-serving little snots who couldn't care less about their parents' rights and feelings as human beings. But there are other times when trust becomes the fall guy, when parents immediately leap into the trust arena even though the conflict may be a difference of style, opinion, or taste instead of a breach of trust.

As you become adept with the techniques described in this book, you'll be able to bring up parents who won't automatically see every issue as one of trust or non-trust. With your help, they'll develop a more sophisticated understanding of this complex concept.

Let's go back through time to those dark ages before you were a kid. Like the day you were born. With good reason, your mom barely gave you womb to maneuver. You were so tiny, dependent, and helpless that you couldn't be trusted to do much of anything except cry and mess up your diapers.

Within minutes of your birth, however, she trusted you enough to cut the cord. Ah, free at last...but look out, before you could say "Waaaaaaa," a new, invisible cord was securely fastened. For years, you were rarely out of your parents' or other adults' sight. On those few occasions when you were left alone to drool contentedly, you were placed in a crib, playpen, or, for those athletes among you, a jolly jumper—always checked frequently to make sure you were A-OK.

As you and your parents matured, the cord was lengthened. Soon you were trusted to crawl around, play in the backyard, and obey your parents' directions to, "Stay right here. I'll only be gone a minute." Since security was way up there on your list of four-year-old must-haves, you stayed right there.

Finally, the great day came when you were five years old and allowed to cross the street by yourself for the first time. For this momentous triumph to occur, your parents had to trust you. They had to believe beyond any doubt that you would look both ways before crossing, wait for a safe opportunity, pay attention, and not daydream or bounce a ball across the street. They had to trust you'd be careful every single time you crossed the street, because just one mistake could turn you into a grisly pancake of crushed bones, smooshed skin, and oozing intestines.

Your parents probably spied on you the first few times you crossed until they became convinced they could trust you. Even then, they worried and worried. (It's one of those things parents do best.) If you managed to make it to your sixth birthday in one piece, chances are your parents added new freedoms to your first-grade lifestyle.

On the other hand, if you became a five-year-old stunt-person-in-training—if you tried to dash between a truck and its shadow, or to meditate yourself across the freeway by closing your eyes and thinking safe thoughts—your parents yanked you back into the crib faster than you could say Seat Belts Save Lives. You waited years before they let you out by yourself again. And when they did, boy, were you watched! You couldn't afford even one little slip-up. You had no trust fund to fall back on.

But let's say you didn't do anything stupid. Even so, the boundaries of your life were clear. Your parents were able (appropriately so) to control most of your activities and to limit your experiences to those areas where their trust was secure. As they gradually came to believe that you were of honest and reliable character, the value of your trust fund increased, providing you with additional credits to use towards expanding your horizons.

Prior to adolescence, the elements of trust were straightforward. Trust could be broken by:

- lying,
- cheating,
- breaking a promise,
- failing to honor a commitment,
- betraying a confidence,
- hurting someone's feelings,
- being careless or irresponsible,
- showing poor judgment, and/or
- being destructive or dangerous.

While each of these reasons still left room for interpretation, chances are that you deserved the trouble you got into when you broke your parents' trust. After all, you were just a little kid.

Now that you're older, though, you bristle at your parents' efforts to control your behavior and impose their standards on you. Sometimes you knowingly break your parents' trust because you don't feel they have a right to make you act according to their values. The fact that trust can be broken intentionally or unintentionally complicates an already tricky issue even further. While damage is done either way, your ability to repair the trust bridge will be greatly influenced by the cause of the breach. It's a lot easier to restore trust that was accidentally betrayed (good faith gone awry) than willfully attacked (bad faith taking its toll).

A trust fund can be unintentionally depleted as the result of:

- confusion,
- misunderstanding,
- false assumptions,
- preoccupations,

- different expectations,
- different values,
- ineffective communication,
- silliness, and/or
- insensitivity.

> *Your parents said, "Be home by eleven," but you would swear on a stack of CDs that they said, "Be home by twelve." That's why you were an hour late.*

> *You were in the middle of the best part of the whole book when your mom asked if you would take your little sister to her dentist appointment later that afternoon. "Sure," you said. But by the time you finished the chapter and wiped away your tears at the dashing Count Musovsky's death at the hands of the evil baron, your promise to help out was long forgotten. That's why you went to the mall.*

While reasons such as these don't excuse the trust-breaking, they do explain it. They explain it in a way that will at least allow you to come across as flaky, distracted, or lovably irresponsible instead of deceitful, selfish, and disobedient. Certainly that's the lesser of two evils.

Ideally, though, you'll want to avoid trust-breaking, period, since bringing up parents who trust you is by far one of the easiest ways to increase your freedom and privileges. You'll want to do everything possible to accumulate the largest, richest, most overflowing trust fund known in the history of home banking. It will pay daily dividends and, if and when something goes wrong, it will be a good cushion against a foreclosure on your freedom.

It should be pretty obvious what you can do to avoid sudden withdrawals from your trust fund as a result of bad-faith actions. Basically, just do the opposite of those things listed in the list before the list before this list:

- Don't lie.
- Don't cheat.
- Don't break promises.
- Don't fail to honor commitments.
- Don't betray confidences.
- Don't hurt feelings.

- Don't be careless or irresponsible.
- Don't show poor judgment.
- Don't be destructive or dangerous.

Avoiding trust breakdowns from accidental betrayal is a much more subtle and sophisticated business. But it can be done. The following strategies will help you to:

1. Minimize those times when trust is unintentionally broken, and
2. Reduce the damage that would otherwise occur.

## Know Thine Enemy

While I'd be the last person to suggest you think of your parents as the enemy, I'd be the first to suggest that you may find yourself in a combative relationship with them from time to time. Reduce conflict by finding out all you can about these people who exert so much influence on your life. Use the techniques outlined on pages 49–65 to discover your parents' sore spots, sensitive issues, and Achilles' heels.

Where do they place their faith in you? What actions inevitably trigger a loss of trust? Where are they irrational, overly protective, easily hurt? With this information, you can identify problem areas before they occur. You can alter your actions or, if that seems out of the question, you can lead your parents to consider your point of view by bringing the matter up in a Problem-Solving Session (see Chapter 5). The more you can learn about your parents, the better equipped you'll be to maneuver strategically to avoid unnecessary conflicts and breakdowns of trust.

## Get Things Clear

Is it that you have to *be home* by midnight or *leave the party* by midnight? Did they say you could have *a friend* over or *a whole bunch of friends* over while they're out of town? Don't assume. Ask!

You may not like the idea of everything being crystal-clear, since it's a well-known fact that teenagers are masterful at using lack of clarity to their advantage. (As in, "But you never said I couldn't!") By not knowing for sure,

you can do things with a semi-clear conscience and a semi-justifiable alibi you suspect you wouldn't be allowed to do if you asked for explicit permission.

While there may be short-term benefits in allowing an unclear situation to exist, this type of activity in the long run will lead your parents to mistrust your judgment. When you exploit lack of clarity, you're playing with fire. You'll receive much more trust by applying your creativity elsewhere. But please, not in the direction of word games.

## Nocturnal Omissions and Other Word Games

Those same teenagers who use vagueness to get what they want are often equally skilled at serving themselves through precision. In this case, it's the meticulous manipulation of the English language. Sins of omission, when combined with startlingly literal interpretations of the mother tongue, can only lead to an erosion of trust. Don't play word games. After all, what possession of yours has greater value than your word?

- **Word Game #1:**

  *"Billy, did you sweep out the garage like I asked?"*

  *"No, Dad, I didn't."*

  *"Why not?"*

  *"I couldn't find the broom."*

  Whew! You're safe as long as Dad doesn't ask:

  *"Did you look for the broom?"*

  *"Uh, not really, I mean, well, I guess, er, no."*

  You were caught. Literally. It'll take more than a broom to sweep up this mess.

- **Word Game #2:**

  *"Alicia, is that liquor I smell on your breath?"*

  "Liquor?" Alicia thinks to herself. "I drank *beer*, not liquor."

73

*"No way, Mom. You couldn't possibly smell liquor on my breath."*

*"Well, I smell something. Have you and your friends been out drinking?"*

Alicia ponders this new challenge. "Hmmm," she thinks, "I was only with *one* friend so I wasn't drinking with *friends*, and we did it *at her house* so I wasn't *out* drinking."

*"No, I haven't been out drinking with friends. Gee, Mom, don't you trust me?"*

Probably not, if this is how Alicia plays word games with her mother. Save your word games for those times when the person you want to protect from hurt is someone other than yourself.

## Go with the Flow

The best way to avoid trust breakdowns resulting from poor communication and erroneous assumptions is to keep talking, to keep a flow of information and feelings between you and your parents at all times.

Have you ever been in a conversation where you and another person both think you're talking about the same thing when, in reality, you've each gone off on a separate track? If you're lucky, the conversation will seem stranger and stranger until one of you says, "Hey, wait a minute, are we talking about the same thing?"

Other times, though, you may never discover the misunderstanding; you may always assume that the two of you were talking about the same subject, and you and your friend will form opinions based on faulty assumptions. This happens all the time between parents and kids. Your parents see the result of an action you take and immediately jump to certain conclusions about your judgment and motivation. They may assume that a conscious decision not to do something was simply your negligence or forgetfulness. They may assume that a joke that came out wrong was your intentional disrespect. They may assume that your justifiable failure to perceive a need was a selfish lack of consideration. Any and all may lead to a raid on your trust fund.

Let your parents know why you did what you did. Don't let them jump to false conclusions. Tell them your reasons. This might uncover a misunderstanding or change the conflict from the issue of your trustworthiness to a

different arena. There may still be a problem, but it could be easier to work it out on another level. If you keep channels open (more about this later), you'll be able to avoid getting a bum rap merely because of miscommunication. And if trouble is deserved, at least you'll get it for the right reason.

## Repairing Damage to the Trust Bridge

Being trustworthy doesn't mean being perfect. You *will* mess up. Ideally, this will be the result of a good-faith error instead of a bad-faith action. When you blow it, you want it to be seen as a fluke, a freak accident that couldn't possibly happen again, and not just one more notch on a long belt of transgressions.

When your trust bridge has come under attack, choose the most appropriate strategy or combination of strategies to keep the structure strong and repair the damage done. Here are seven for you to try:

1.  Use Active Listening (see Chapter 4) to understand your parents' position. This shows them that you *accept* their right to have feelings and opinions, even though you may not *agree*.

2.  Use I-messages (see Chapter 4) to tell them your thoughts and feelings. This will encourage them to *accept* your point of view and your right to have it, even though they may not *agree*.

3.  Apologize, admit an error, or use the "You're Absolutely Right" technique (see Chapter 4).

4.  Commit an Act of Goodness (see Chapter 3). Breaking someone's trust is like taking something from them. If the Lord can giveth and taketh, surely you, who tooketh, can giveth back.

5.  Undo any practical consequences of your action. Can you buy a new one, repair an old one, clean it up, dry it out, write a note, make a call, try again? Do whatever you can to reverse the damage.

6.  Check assumptions! Straighten out any remaining confusion or lack of clarity that might have contributed to the trust-breaking in the first place.

7.  Don't repeat the action.

Trust is a cycle.  The more trustworthy you are, the more you are trusted.  A positive momentum is established that carries you over the rough spots and brings greater freedom and responsibilities your way.  Your folks get used to seeing examples of your trustworthiness, and that's what they look for.  Mistrust creates momentum, too, except it's a negative momentum.  Your parents see all the times you break their trust, and that's what they look for.

If there's already a negative trust cycle in your family, you'll need to discover the cause.  It could be that you or your parents simply may not deserve to be trusted.  Your actions may more than justify the feelings of mistrust.  Nothing will change until behaviors change.  Or there may be hidden issues at work; perhaps your parents have fears that prevent them from extending trust.  Those fears will have to be addressed before change can happen.

Trust-breaking can also be used as a weapon, a way of getting back at someone.  Or it may be that trust doesn't exist because there is no self-trust.  If you know that you sometimes lie or steal or cheat, how can you trust that someone else won't?

Being able to trust and be trusted is essential to bringing up parents who accept and respect you.  Once you've absorbed all the ideas in this book, you'll be able to make educated guesses as to the cause of any mistrust in your household.  Then you'll be able to decide how best to attack the problem—whether to search for hidden agendas, initiate Problem-Solving Sessions (see Chapter 5), shape up your own actions, gather intelligence, make contracts, or offer love.  While you're at it, you might as well throw into the pot two other concepts that go with trust like ketchup goes with French fries:  namely, freedom and responsibility.

# YOUR FREEDOM: THEIR RESPONSIBILITY

The word "responsibility" is so overused that you don't know what it means anymore.  You do know it's a big item on your parents' agenda; you know it's a condition to which your livelihood is attached; and you know its absence does not make your parents' hearts grow fonder.

*"That was a very irresponsible thing to do."*

*"How can we trust you when you're so irresponsible?"*

*"Until you show a little more responsibility around here, you can forget about staying out late on weekends."*

If you want to bring up parents who will let you do what you want, responsibility will have to be a big item on your agenda, too.

Think of responsibility as a subset of trust. If trust is broad and a bit abstract—if trust applies to your character, virtues, and values, if it's a basic belief in your worthiness as a human being who is honest, caring, and straight with people—then responsibility, the way your parents see it, has to do with your practical skills for interacting with the world. Thus, within certain limits, it is possible to have your parents' trust while being irresponsible in a few areas. You could be the most reliable, decent soul on a person-to-person level, yet, when it came to being on time, or returning something you borrowed, or driving a car, you could be a real flake.

Naturally, you want to have both your parents' trust and their faith in your responsibility. If you spent most of your time lost in Space Cadet City, you'd find yourself receiving fewer and fewer privileges and freedoms. This is due to one of the mathematical constants in the universe: the Parent's Law of Direct Proportionality Between Freedom and Responsibility. What it means is that the more responsible you are, the more willing your parents will be to entrust you with the perks of adult life: cars, money, mobility, independence, decision-making.

There's no way around this law, for the inescapable fact is that your parents are ultimately responsible for you and your actions. You may not like it that way, and they may not like it that way, but our current society makes it that way.

- If *you* cause an accident, *they* can be sued.
- If *you* skip school, *they* can be fined.
- If *you* break a neighbor's plate glass window, *they* have to pay.

Now, your parents may turn around and transfer the burden of such consequences to you, but that doesn't eliminate their primary responsibility for you in the eyes of society and the law.

Sometimes you are the sole recipient of the results of your own irre-sponsibility. If you forget your homework, you're the one who has to stay after school; if you forget to meet a friend as promised, you're the one on the receiving end of his or her anger. Many parents, however, like to barge right in and claim responsibility for vast areas of your life that could be left in your hands. Homework, for instance. How you do in school. How you dress, even how you interact with friends. They do this for three reasons:

1. Because they love you, they feel it's their responsibility to see that you're responsible and perfect and wonderful (even when you could make a good case that it's none of their business).

2. Your behavior reflects upon their image.

3. In some cases, sooner or later, they'll be forced (because of the law or their love) to join you in the penalties of your less-than-responsible actions.

Let's say they think that the way you ride your skateboard is irresponsible. "You're too reckless," they warn. The way you look at it, it's your body, your bones, your blood, and your business. If you have an accident, you'll pay the price...but they'll have to pay the medical bills. It's nearly impossible to elim-inate them from the equation.

It'll be a long time until you're completely responsible for your own life, your own support and actions. When you're 30 years old, you can skateboard any way you like because you'll be on your own. Until then, you've got to deal with the notion that your freedom is their responsibility.

Some kids (certainly not you) take advantage of this fact. They allow themselves to be careless and irresponsible because they know their parents have to bail them out—sometimes literally! It's hard to imagine that these kids will ever gain from this type of ploy.

*"Okay, okay. Enough already. I'll be responsible and I'll get my freedom. Next chapter."*

Not so fast. Definitions of responsible behavior can shift depending on a person's values and priorities. Conflict can develop because what you think is responsible behavior doesn't even come close to what your parents think. Watch.

*You thought it was wise and mature to decide to drive your friend's car since he had been drinking. You hadn't had a drop. So what if you only had a learner's permit? That's just a technicality in the face of life and death! Your parents were speechless at what they saw as poor judgment and irresponsibility.*

*You thought skipping school to comfort a hysterical friend who just found out she was pregnant was a humanitarian act and a courageous statement of values. Your parents (and teachers) thought it was the height of irresponsibility.*

*You thought, as you swept up the broken glass, that stacking all the glasses on one tray while clearing the table was a risk worth taking in the pursuit of efficiency. Your parents were furious that you were so careless with their belongings.*

Since humans have different philosophies of life and place different values on the importance of people, possessions, punctuality, and practical competence, doesn't it follow that you and your parents are going to come up against different interpretations of your actions and decisions? You bet it does.

So what's a poor, freedom-lovin' kid to do? Look, you already know a lot of the items upon which your parents judge responsibility:

- Being on time.
- Doing chores.
- Cleaning up after yourself.
- Taking care of your possessions.
- Meeting obligations.
- Being safe and careful.
- Thinking of others.

Where your experience and common sense have defined responsible behavior, just follow through with your best instincts. Seventy-five percent of the time, you and your parents will probably see eye-to-eye on the issue, and you'll both make the same judgments. But what about the other 25 percent of the time? If you disagree even once in every four situations, that's a lot of conflict! Just a glance at the above list suggests all sorts of areas ripe for the harvesting of different interpretations.

Being safe and careful, for example. What constitutes a reasonable risk versus a foolish one? Where can the immortality you envision for yourself and the doom your parents see around every corner find happy and realistic reconciliation?

How about taking care of your possessions? Do your parents seem obsessively concerned with material things? (Perhaps because they paid for them?) Do you, in your search for a higher spirituality, come across to them as spoiled and indifferent?

How about meeting obligations? In what order? At what cost? What happens when obligations conflict? When something unexpected comes up and a choice must be made? How do you decide what's most important?

Once again, I don't bring up these intricacies to provide you with excuses.

*"Well, Mother, I'm not irresponsible, you just think I am, based upon your archaic and myopic value system."*

No indeed. Responsibility is a real thing. It can be felt, heard, observed, and smelled. (Like when you forget to take out the garbage.) You know it exists. Think how you'd feel if your parents suddenly renounced their responsibilities towards you. No food in the house, no financial support, no rides, no tuition, no medical care. The world would fall apart if people didn't act responsibly.

What can you do to keep your world from falling apart, to minimize the chances that you'll be seen as an irresponsible kid? Here are some tips for you to try:

1. ***Get things clear.*** Be sure that you and your parents recognize existing limits, rules, and expectations to mean the same thing.

2. ***Make lists of agreed-upon responsibilities.*** Post them if you'd like. There'll be no question whether Tuesday is your night for dishes or rubbish, whether tying up the newspapers is something you do for extra money or as part of your chores.

3. ***Make contracts.*** Write out the precise understandings, obligations, and conditions underlying agreements and commitments between you and your folks.

4. ***Come up with a schedule.*** This is an especially good idea for those space cadets among you who forget they have music lessons on Wednesdays and orthodontist appointments on Thursdays after school. Of course, if you're that flaky, you may forget to look at your schedule. Accordingly, those of you inhabiting the really distant galaxies might consider enlisting the help of a friend or sibling to give a reminder.

5. ***When in doubt, check it out.*** Why risk trouble just because of confusion or misunderstanding? Ask and ye shall find out.

6. ***Observe your behavior.*** Often there are patterns to a person's irresponsible behaviors. Analyze yourself. Do you tend to goof up only in certain areas? If so, why? What's going on? If allergy appointments are the only appointments you forget, maybe you're afraid of shots. See? If you can discover patterns, you can find solutions.

7. ***Write yourself a note.*** Leave it in a place so obvious that it screams to be noticed.

8. ***Do it NOW.*** A lot of irresponsibility is good, old-fashioned forgetfulness—a slippage of the mind. The longer you put something off, the greater the chances you'll forget or something else will come along to entice you away. Get it over with, whether it's a chore, a phone call, a practice session, or an appointment. You'll feel much better without something hanging over you.

9. ***Take the bull by the horns.*** Be active. Don't let problems occur through passivity or inattention. Responsibility exists; look for it, talk about it, and ask your parents to be specific when they accuse you of irresponsibility.

10. ***Give advance notice.*** Anticipate problems so you can work them out ahead of time. If you agreed to babysit your little brother next Friday night and you've just been invited to a party at the same time, don't wait until Friday afternoon to say you can't babysit. Bring it up as early as you can. You'll avoid looking irresponsible and inconsiderate, and you'll increase the chances that plans can be changed.

    Style is important here. You don't want to give the impression that you make and take commitments lightly. On the other hand, it's reasonable to expect that the unexpected will occur, that people will change their minds or want to alter prior commitments. Look far ahead, anticipate the possible consequences of your actions or inactions, and assume the responsibility for working things through so no one will be hurt. If you can be responsible about predicting your irresponsibility, you'll be in great shape.

11. ***Get in trouble for a good reason.*** If you're going to be labeled irresponsible, try to be irresponsible on a high plane of behavior—one where you take an action based on careful consideration, high principle, and integrity. It's a little like civil disobedience; your values compel you to a certain position, even when you know there will be consequences to suffer.

    Be sure your parents realize that the course you charted was a conscious choice and not mindless stupidity. Agree to disagree. At least then your parents can say, "We respect you for wanting to follow your own principles, but we still think what you did was irresponsible." You'll feel much better when they dock your allowance for the next three weeks.

12. ***Make that call.*** When you don't turn up on schedule, it's parent nature to assume the worst: you've been raped, run over, kidnapped, murdered, mugged, or drugged. By the time you get home, your parents will be so concerned about their beloved little precious that they'll be ready to kill you.

All of this can be avoided with one phone call. Assuming that your lateness, on at least a few occasions, is the result of factors beyond your control (car problems, class kept late, illness, someone else kept you waiting), prevent unwarranted charges of irresponsibility by letting your parents know what's up. This doesn't mean you're a baby checking in. It means you're smart enough to know what's in your best interests, which in this case happens to be happily coincidental with your parents' best interests. So make that call.

If you were irresponsible for less than respectable reasons—if you simply lost track of time, for example—call anyway. Far better to say, "Mom, I totally forgot, I lost track of time, I know I'm late, I'm leaving right now and I'll be home in half an hour," than to show up as if nothing happened. At least you will have succeeded in eliminating a half-hour in which your parents would otherwise be planning your demise.

Since making that call is such an indispensable maneuver, here's one last thought: If the emergency quarter you keep for this purpose has a way of getting spent on other emergencies (like candy and video games), you needn't fret. You can call home collect, even if it's a local call. It's a small price to pay (for whoever ends up paying) to keep you in the clear.

# Chapter 3

# TRICKS AND TREATS

**H**istory abounds with examples of shining altruism in the pursuit of personal gain. Whether it's the United States bestowing a token $3 billion on a foreign country or a daughter washing the family car without being told, the use of well-chosen generosity and clever planning to get what you want is easily as old as your parents.

There's nothing immoral or dishonest about the ploys—er, strategies—contained in this chapter. They have withstood the test of time and have been used successfully by millions of teenagers. The fact that you may have a motive up your ulterior doesn't diminish the benefits conveyed upon your parents by the practice of these methods.

Study these ideas carefully. Choose the ones that will work best in your particular family. Use them with discretion; overuse can dull even the sharpest blade.

# IT'S ABOUT TIME

If you want to keep on tickin' without taking a lickin', you'll need to master the fine art of precision timing. Your parents are already aware of the importance of timing. Why else would they say, "There's a right time and a wrong time for everything"?

The problem is, they seem to recognize only the wrong times. And some other time. Or maybe next time. While you're thinking showtime, they're thinking bedtime. For the time being, however, we'll let your folks worry about those moments when it's time to settle down and shape up. As for you, it's high time you realized that for once, your folks are correct. There *is* a right time and a wrong time for everything, especially when it comes to getting what you want from your parents.

You can increase the "yes's" and decrease the "no's" if you learn to choose the right moment to pop the question.

## Good Times to Ask for Something

- When it's your parents' payday.
- When your parents are relaxed, cheerful, unpressured.
- When you are relaxed, cheerful, unpressured.
- When your parents are in an affectionate, supportive, and accepting mood.
- When your parents are alone and are not going to be influenced by what their peers will think.
- When your trust fund is well-endowed.
- When you've been responsible, well-behaved, and worthy in your parents' eyes of having your request fulfilled.

Only you know when the best times can be found in your household. Perhaps before dinner, when your folks are unwinding. Or after dinner, when things have settled down. Or in the middle of a lazy, refreshing weekend. Do your intelligence work so you'll know when you're most likely to encounter a receptive parent target. By the same token, be on the lookout for...

## Bad Times to Ask for Something

- When your folks are rushed or distracted.
- When your folks are burdened with problems of their own.
- When your folks feel unloved and abused by their children.
- When there's an audience whose presence may adversely affect your parents' decision.
- When there's already an ill wind blowing in your direction.
- When calamity has struck or is about to strike, as in relatives coming to visit, illness, or financial reversals.
- When it's a few days before your parents' payday.

## A Note for Sophisticated Time-Peepers

The particular dynamics of your family may suggest times when exceptions to the above rules are appropriate. For example, a harried or distracted parent is generally a poor target for a request. Too often, the answer is "no" just to be done with it. You may discover, however, that your folks, when hassled, are just as likely to say "yes" to be done with it. If so, go for it—carefully.

Similarly, while most parents tend to get even more parental in front of other adults, if you know your parents and their friends well, you may find it advantageous to pop a question in the presence of others. Your parents might answer more generously, tolerantly, or liberally with certain friends looking on. Peer pressure, you know.

When it comes to timing, there are no absolutes. Every family's schedules, rhythms, and interactions are different. While the broad guidelines for good and bad timing outlined here generally hold true, be alert to those unique opportunities in your home when the bell can be made to toll for you.

# BOOK 'EM

Give your parents a book on parenting. Ideally, it should be written by someone whose name is followed by a lot of initials. This indicates that the author combines the best of the medical and corporate worlds, thereby increasing

the chances that your parents will pay attention. M.D., Ph.D., Ed.D., M.B.A., P.C., Inc., and Ltd. would be adequate for starters.

Naturally, care should be exercised in the choice of book to ensure that it matches your own philosophy of parenting. It just wouldn't do for your folks to stumble on *Go to Your Room: A Parent's Guide to Keeping Kids in Line* by I.M. Meany, Ph.D. and B. So whatever book you choose, be sure to preview it. Lord knows how impressionable parents can be. You wouldn't want them to get hold of the wrong kind of material.

# WHAT, ME APOLOGIZE?

There are three basic types of apology: the Before, the During, and the After. Each has its moment.

The Before apology is best used when you see trouble around the next bend. The idea is to soften the blow, to beat your parents to the punch with your name on it.

> *"Dad, can I talk to you?" (Always a good opener. Makes Dad feel you know he exists.)*

> *"Sure. What's up?"*

> *"You know the calculator you lent me?"*

> *"Yeah. "*

> *"I'm really sorry, but I accidentally left it on the bus. I went back to look but it was gone. I'm really sorry. I'll get you a new one."*

> *"Oh, don't worry about it. I got it for free when I made a deposit at the bank. I bet we can get another one. "*

> *"Whew. I was really worried. Sorry again."*

> *"That's all right. And thanks for letting me know."*

Contrast that to the more typical scenario.

> *"Oh, God, I lost my dad's calculator. He's gonna kill me if he finds out. Maybe he'll forget I had it."*

*Several days pass...*

*"Timmy, where's my calculator? I need it right away."*

*"Er, Dad, I, uh...."*

*"What is it?"*

*"I, er, well, I sort of lost it."*

*"You what?!? How could you lose it?"*

*"Well, it just happened, I didn't mean—"*

*"You are so irresponsible! Can't you take care of other people's things? That's the last time I'll lend you anything of mine."*

*"I'm sorry Dad, really."*

*"Sorry? Hmpph. It's a little late to be sorry."*

Yes, it is. Had Timmy been sorry a few days earlier, this might have been avoided.

The During apology is generally not heard too well, but it can serve to keep the lid on once a problem has occurred. Note the dramatic use of this apology form in saving this kid's skin:

*"Young lady, it is two in the morning. Where have you been? You were supposed to be home at midnight."*

*"I know, but they mixed up the reels and had to rewind the film and then we got out late and missed the last bus so we had to walk."*

*"Walk!! You walked home from the plaza? At night? Do you know how dangerous that is? Why didn't you call?"*

*"I didn't want to wake you."*

*"Wake us? How could we sleep wondering whether you were lying in some ditch? What do you have to say for yourself?"*

*"I'm sorry. I didn't mean to worry you. I'll be sure to call next time."*

*"Next time? I'm not sure if there will be a next time. Unless you show more responsibility...."*

*"Really, Dad, I'm sorry. I just wasn't thinking."*

*"All right. It's late and we should both go to sleep. I just wish you'd think a little more about...."*

Dad may sputter on for a while, but you've managed to take the sails out of his wind. Had an apology not been offered, this argument might still be going on. The best thing to do in the thick of a crisis is to keep cool and stick to the guns of your apology. This is precisely *not* the time to hook in and argue. This is *not* the time to defend yourself by blaming the theater, the bus company, the phone company for charging 25 cents which you didn't have (see Make That Call in Chapter 2), and it's especially *not* the time to blame your father. Somehow I don't think he wants to hear, "If you didn't set such an early curfew, I wouldn't be late and we wouldn't be having this fight." Use the During apology to cut your losses.

Finally, the *pièce de résistance* of apologies, the After. When used correctly, this has the effect of turning the lemon of your error into the lemonade of your redemption. Here's how to use it:

*The bad news has already gone down. You had a horrible, door-slamming, screaming match with your mother in the morning while she drove you to school. You can't even remember what it was about. She probably made one of those remarks halfway between parental concern and parental interference and you, bristling, snapped back quite ferociously.*

*It's now late afternoon. Mom is back from work and enough time has passed to cool you down and turn your mother's anger into philosophical maternal mellowness.*

*"Oh, well," she sighs to herself, "no one ever said adolescence would be easy. Maybe I shouldn't have criticized him like that."*

*Now is your moment to make hay while the son shines.*

*"Mom," say you sweetly, "I'm sorry about this morning."*

*Your mother turns, a bit surprised by the unexpected apology, and feels the warm flow of forgiving motherly juices.*

*"Why, Richie," she smiles, coming over to give you a big hug, "that's very nice of you to say. I'm sorry, too."*

Instead of the hot-tempered, foul-mouthed kid of the morning, you are now, in your mom's eyes, golden. Your apology means that you must have thought things over, and your mom sees a maturity and a sensitivity in you that brings a smile to her heart. Like the bone that grows stronger after a break, your relationship with your mom has mended from this fracture with greater respect and affection for all. It is better to have argued and apologized than never to have argued at all.

Almost.

On the other hand, you may be thinking, "Why should I say I'm sorry? I'm not! She started it! I'm not sorry for what I said. She deserved it!" Here is where the beauty of language and literalness comes in. Note that our wayward teenager only says, "Mom, I'm really sorry about this morning." While Mom is won over by the apology, he never really explains what he's sorry *for*. His behavior? The words he said? The fact that his feelings were hurt? That his mother got upset? That it happened at all? Or was he sorry that the morning was gray and drizzly?

We don't know, and for the purposes at hand, it doesn't matter. The point is that the statement can be phrased in such a way to be true to the apology-giver and the apology-receiver. Teenagers hate to apologize for something if they're not sorry. The key is to find something you are sorry about and to focus on that. This need not violate the adolescent code of honor.

It's even acceptable to include within the apology a silent clause intended for your ears only:

*"Mom, I'm really sorry I upset you this morning."* (Although I had every right to say what I did.)

*"Mom, I'm sorry we had a fight."* (Although you started it.)

*"Mom, I'm really sorry about this morning."* ('Cause it sure ruined my day.)

Smart as you are, and assuming that you've read Chapter 2, you're probably wondering, "Wait a minute.... Isn't this the same as playing word games?" No. You're telling the truth. You *are* sorry the fight took place. In word games, your motivation is to deceive your parents to avoid getting into trouble. Here your motivation is to make your mom feel better. What she hears is the apology, and that's what matters.

Be judicious in apologizing. The worst thing you can do is cheapen the technique through overuse. You don't want to give the impression that you think it's okay to mess up as long as you say you're sorry. Limit the times you mess up so you won't have to bludgeon this fine approach into early oblivion.

# COMMIT AN ACT OF GOODNESS

An Act of Goodness is only effective (and full of integrity) if committed when you don't want anything in return. By doing something kind for your folks, you're investing in a savings account of good will that you can draw on at a later time, when you do want something.

What, exactly, is an Act of Goodness? Simply put, it's any kind, generous, unexpected action that is not one of your regular responsibilities. Acts of Goodness include my favorite, the Offer to Help. A well-chosen offer to help produces the proverbial effect of having your cake and eating it, too. This is due to the fact that parents *love* offers to help and can be so delighted by your spontaneous generosity that they will wish to reward you by declining your assistance.

*"Hi, Mom,"* you say on the wing as you head towards the door.

*(Pause.)*

*"Do you want some help with those dishes before I go out?"*

*"Why, aren't you sweet. I'm almost through, but thank you anyway. You run along."*

*"Okay. Bye, Mom."*

This offer went just according to plan. You must, however, be prepared to follow through if your offer is accepted. Clever timing is a plus. Note that in this example, Mom was just finishing up. Had she responded "Yes, I want some help," the dishes could have been washed quickly, sending you along with minimum delay. With practice, you'll learn to adjust your timing to your affinity for the task, to your schedule, and to how badly you want whatever it is you're not going to let on you want. (At least, not for a few days.)

Remember, an Act of Goodness immediately followed by a request for something isn't generous. It's tacky. Since many of you will not be familiar with this technique, here are four tips to quickly bring you up to snuff:

1. **Focus** on the image you want to create in your parents' eyes: an image of unselfish cooperation, cheerful altruism, and unstinting participation in family responsibilities.

2. **Look** for a need and fill it. The dishes need doing, the dog needs bathing, the laundry needs folding, the rug needs vacuuming.

3. **Listen** for a need and fill it. Not only will you get points for an Act of Goodness, but you'll also earn Bonus Points since your parents will be pleased to know that you actually listened to them. This confirms their existence, which is something all parents need from time to time.

   *"I don't know when I'll get the time to trim the hedges,"* bemoans *Dad one day.*

   *Quick, there's your cue! Or....*

   *You overhear your mom talking to your little sister.*

   *"Sally, I've told you, as soon as I have an afternoon free I'll go shopping with you."*

   *Enter you, stage right.*

   *"I'll take her, Mom."*

   *Bravo!*

4. **Keep** a list handy so you can generate a backlog of Acts of Goodness. Some Acts that are almost always welcome (remember, they can't be part of your normal routine):

- Wash the family car.  (It could be yours someday.)
- Do extra yard work.
- Vacuum.  Clean a floor.
- Play with a little sibling.  (Get him or her out of Mom or Dad's way.)
- Write a letter to a grandparent.  (While not strictly a direct Act of Goodness, the benefit to your parents comes when Granny or Gramps receives the letter, calls your parents, and expounds on how wonderful you are and what a wonderful job they must be doing to bring up a person as wonderful as you to have written them such a wonderful letter. This, in case you haven't guessed, is a real good one.)
- Help with the laundry.
- For one whole day, don't play your music where it can be heard.

The list could go on, but I suspect that some of you may be feeling faint from this sudden overdose of kind intentions.  Use your imagination and powers of observation.  You'll never be at a loss for new ideas.

# Breakfast in Bed

This Act of Goodness merits special mention. In the lore of American culture, Breakfast in Bed (sometimes referred to by its acronymically appropriate nickname, BIB) has achieved stature of mythic proportions. It represents a luxurious pinnacle of civilized living that all parents covet and most never experience, especially if they have teenagers in the household.

The nature of BIB suggests that it is a weekend phenomenon. This allows parents to linger and enjoy the full flush of Sunday morning sleep-in-ed-ness. This also explains why BIB is such a rare occurrence; after all, how many teenagers are up before lunchtime on weekends to fix it? Nevertheless, don't miss out on this warmly symbolic opportunity for advancement, even if it means setting an alarm clock for the ungodly hour of ten in the morning.

"I love you Mom."

"I love you, too, Justin, but the answer is still no!"

"But I can't cook," you say. So much the better. The whole point of BIB is to provide your parents with an unaccustomed standard of luxury. Fortunately, gastronomical elitism can be eaten raw. Fresh orange juice. You can squeeze, can't you? Can you shop? Good. Concentrate on the special touches. Buy some fresh strawberries. And cream. (Use the cream for coffee; it's a step above the milk they usually have.) Or warm the milk for *café au lait*.

Can you turn on the oven? Great. Heat some croissants. Serve with butter or jam. Toast some bagels if you're not in a Gallic mood. Lay out a tastefully arranged platter of cream cheese, lox or kippers, onions, lettuce, tomato. You're not cooking, you're creating edible art. If you happen to be the Julia Child of junior high school and want to whip up purée of cantaloupe soup (chilled, of course), Eggs Florentine, escalloped potatoes with smoked salmon, cinnamon sweet rolls, and chocolate cointreau cheese cake, hey, go for it.

Use the best china, the finest silverware, and linen napkins if you can find them. How can your parents complain? Your choice only reflects the high esteem in which you hold them. If they make gurgling sounds and look faint as Grandma's heirloom teapot teeters on the tray, you can silence them with an innocent smile and the words, "Nothing but the best for the people I love!"

It's only fair—and should establish your firm claim on sainthood—to include clean-up in your goodness. However, most parents will leap to those chores themselves. It's a way of rewarding your beneficence, as well as lowering the odds on damage to that teapot.

For the final touches, bring in the Sunday newspaper, put their favorite record on the stereo, and leave them alone. (This way they'll be free to sing your praises and do whatever it is parents do in bed on Sunday mornings.)

The logistics and cost of Breakfast in Bed may recommend this as a multi-sibling endeavor. Share the wealth.

## Parents' Day Off

Announce to your parents that you're going to give them a day off. If that taxes your goodness too severely, how about an evening off, or a half-day's vacation? Your job during that period is to assume all responsibilities that would otherwise be theirs: cooking, laundry, diaper changing, cleaning, babysitting, doorbell answering, whatever. This frees them to sleep, read, play,

see a movie, go out, and marvel upon what a good kid you are. The more time you give them, the more time they have to marvel. How marvelous for you!

CAUTION: Be realistic about the extent to which you can take over. If your sister has to be driven to soccer practice and you're 13, I wouldn't recommend that you assume this responsibility. If you can't ride bikes or take the bus, you'll have to let your parents drive her. There will still be ample time for them to luxuriate in the hassle-free holiday you have so generously provided.

# PRESENTS OF MINE:
# ADVANCED GIFT-GIVING

Unlike Acts of Goodness, where your gift is in the form of a service rendered, and unlike Breakfast in Bed and Parents' Days Off, which justify their own definitions, gift-giving is simply the offering of a tangible object designed to express your warm affection for the 'rents.

Remember the cardinal rule of gift-giving: You can't ask for anything after giving the gift. If you give your parents a present and they feel touched, that's called a good deed. If you give your parents a present and then ask for something you want, that's called a bribe. Only long after you've established yourself as an unselfish, caring young philanthropist can you ask for things you want close to the moment of gift-giving. Then it's not called a bribe, it's called a coincidence.

You know best what your parents would like to receive. That's what to give. It could be a tool, a book, a CD, a pipe, a scarf, a rakish beret. It could be an I.O.U. for an evening of babysitting or an afternoon of snow-shoveling. Try not to give perfume. Most mothers have been gifted with more perfume by the time their kids are 12 than the Dallas Cowboys cheerleaders could use in a lifetime.

But there are never enough flowers. Everyone loves flowers. Even your father (although it may take another 20 years of social progress before he can come out of the garden and admit it). Buy flowers, send flowers. No money? No problem. Cut wildflowers. (They're not wild if they're in your neighbor's yard.)

If you a) don't like store-bought presents, b) are plumb out of moola, or c) are just plain cheap, you can always make something. Parents adore the products of their children's cottage industries. Make a planter box, a set of coasters, a piece of pottery, a painting. Don't make a mess.

A written greeting, on the other hand, is always in fashion. When in doubt, a card will shout, "I love you, Mom, I love you, Dad!" You can't go wrong with a handmade statement of your fond feelings. Draw a picture, pen a poem, tell 'em they're the greatest.

*Roses are red,*
*Violets are blue,*
*If you weren't my folks,*
*I'd go boo-hoo.*

Or how about:

*Roses are red,*
*Carnations are white,*
*Hey Mom, Hey Dad,*
*It's been over an hour since our last fight.*
*Love ya.*

Take your time. Thirty years from now, Mom will still shed a tear when she pulls your yellowed card from that special place in the bottom of her jewelry box and remembers her generous, creative, and loving little baby. What she won't remember is the request for a new sweater that came several days later.

# SIBLINGS TO THE RESCUE

Surely siblings have a higher calling in life than mere annoyance. (Where would Orville have been without Wilbur?) The skillful use of the sibling alliance is a true challenge to your creative parent-raising. The possibilities are as endless as the last lecture you got. Here are just a few of the ways in which brothers and sisters can be transformed from nuisances into necessities.

## The Sibling as Shoulder
## on Which to Cry

Sometimes you've just gotta talk. Instead of getting into another fight with *el parentos*, let off your steam by tirading to an understanding sibling. It's safe, pollution-free, and you'll feel better without risking further furies.

## The Sibling as Board
## on Which to Sound

Siblings are a repository for good advice. They may have already tried it, done it, gone through it, or botched it. Use their experience to your advantage. Remember:

- A wise kid makes mistakes.
- A wiser kid learns from mistakes.
- The wisest kid of them all learns from siblings' mistakes.

## The Sibling as Spy

I'm not talking about covert actions here. You wouldn't want your little sister to listen through doors, peek in keyholes, or search through drawers. You could do all that yourself. The idea is to use her as an *overt* agent.

She can maneuver where you still fear to tread. She can get the lay of the land for you. Maybe you were sent to your room; maybe you're not sure if it's safe to reappear; maybe you want to find out if your parents have cooled off or are still plotting a premature end to your existence. Big Sis or Little Sis can mingle freely with the targets and bring back intelligence you can use in formulating your apology, your approach, or your escape.

# United We Stand:
# The Power of Collective Bargaining

This is the old "strength in numbers" bit. It's based upon the following premise: You can fool one of the siblings some of the time, but you can't fool all of the siblings any of the time. Some situations cry out for the call-up of all sibling troops. While you may be the only one on the hot seat, a threat to all your livelihoods could well exist. If one should fall, can the others be far behind? It'll be a lot harder for your parents to overrule all of you than one of you.

Beware, though. When parents get backed into a corner, they can be most inventive in marshalling their own forces. It's possible that this ploy can backfire, and you might pull your siblings into your own peck of trouble. If that happens, don't despair. Misery loves company, and now you have lots of both.

## The Sibling as Special Envoy

A highly sophisticated use of sibling supportiveness. Get your brother or sister to take your case directly to the Ancient Ones. It is important that he or she not appear to be on your side as much as on the side of peace and reconciliation. If viewed as a neutral proponent of good faith and family harmony, the chosen sibling can be most effective in asking your parents to reconsider a decision, reassess a punishment, or restore a privilege.

For example, your sib can give your parents information on a "just-between-us, you-may-not-know-that-Freddy-was-cut-from-the-swim-team-today-and-is-kinda-upset-which-is-why-he-kicked-the-ball-that-accidentally-went-through-the-patio-window" basis. Discuss ahead of time with your sibling the points to get across, the defense to be presented, the solution to propose, and the questions to ask. It may take several hours if not days of domestic shuttle diplomacy before success can be concluded. Be patient.

# BOO-HOO

Very powerful. Naturally, it works best if public crying is a rare activity for you. You wouldn't want to cry wolf with this approach. (Private crying is another matter. You should feel free to do that to your heart's—and tear ducts'—content.)

The secret to creative crying is this: You must make it look like you're trying not to cry but just can't help it. While your intellect is willing to accept your parents' "no," your heart cannot; the pain and disappointment are too great. Stoic that you are, you're still human, and the aching wellspring of hurt bubbling from the depths of your soul exerts a pressure too great to resist. But, of course, you don't want to upset your parents by letting on how profound your anguish really is. (Actually, you do, but it can't look like that.)

So keep your eyes big and wide, like a loving puppy.

Look straight at the offending parent.

Allow your eyes to fill just enough to make your parent sense impending sadness on your part.

When you can hold it no longer (or need to get on with it because you're meeting a friend), let one tear roll down your tender child's cheek.

When you're sure it's been noticed, wipe it away as if you didn't want anyone to see.

Immediately produce two more tears, this time one from each eye. A genteel snort or winsome sniffle can't hurt.

Chances are excellent that your suffering, so long as it appears unintended, will draw your parent into a more empathetic and compromising mood. The key is to make it look as if showing the extent of your agony is the last thing you'd want to do.

CAUTION: Avoid overt sobbing and heaving. That your parents can write off as adolescent over-emotionalism. The checked tear, on the other hand, is much loftier. When exercised as a high art form, it should qualify you for sympathy based upon your parents' recognition that you are in the grip of existential angst and Jungian despair common to the human condition.

# FAMILY FUN

The two need not be mutually exclusive. Look at it this way: You and your folks are busy all day. You've got school, sports, lessons, homework, chores. They've got work, appointments, household errands, family responsibilities. How much time is left when you and your parents finally get together? Do I hear you say "almost none," "very little," and "practically zilch"?

And how do you spend the little time you do have together? Arguing, yelling, fighting, nagging, criticizing? Quality Time it is not. Quarreling Time is more like it.

Another destructive cycle has been created. The more you pick at each other, the less you like each other; the less you like each other, the more you pick at each other, and the less time you want to spend together. Pretty soon, 100 percent of your family interactions could be unpleasant, even though they occupy a small fraction of the day.

Families need to spend time together just *having fun*. I know that spending Saturday night with your family may not be your idea of fun. That's all right; it's not mine, either. What I'm talking about is the creation of some positive moments in your family interactions. No wonder you fight all the time if you only see and call up the negative in one another.

Break the cycle. Shoot for the positive. Even if it's only for 15 minutes a day, make a point of having a good time with your parents. Do something that you'd all enjoy. It could be something special or something ordinary made special. Choose an activity that safely avoids current conflicts. Don't go for a ride if your parents' driving drives you crazy. Don't play croquet if you can't stand losing. (Or if your father can't stand losing.) Find something neutral and pleasurable.

- Play ping-pong.
- Go for a family walk.
- Bake a cake.
- Play a game.
- Go canoeing.
- Watch a video.
- Share a hobby.
- Take an ice-cream break.

It's not as though I'm asking you to move in with them or anything as horrible as that. I'm just asking you to spend a few minutes together, happily engaged.

Positive family time is helpful because:

- It shows that you can spend time together without fighting.
- You'll be more likely to notice each other's good qualities.
- Each successful occasion reinforces good feelings; the negative cycle gets broken.
- You may actually discover that you like and enjoy one another's company when you're not squabbling.
- Critical remarks may diminish if your parents see your faults (and you see theirs) in a larger picture that includes virtues as well.

CAUTION: Family vacations are an entirely different kettle of contention. If you can spend a whole week in close quarters with your family and without the comforts of home and still have a great time together, more power to you! Do it as often as you can. For many families, though, vacations are terrible. Tensions only multiply as unrealistic expectations are shattered. Nosy relatives, more intimate contact, and less privacy create extra opportunities to notice and catch up on fault-finding. By the end of the trip, a week of fun has turned into a nightmare of getting on each other's nerves.

If this sounds familiar, some of these ideas might help next time the black cloud of a vacation looms over your family's future:

1. Bring a good friend along. You'll be happier and family friction could be lessened.
2. Escalate your Acts of Goodness during the trip as a preventive measure.
3. Bring lots of things to keep you busy: books, magazines, cassette tapes, musical instruments, fingerpaints, the collected works of Proust, whatever.
4. Plan your vacation days so that you and your folks can have private time.
5. Have a friendly Problem-Solving Session (see Chapter 5) before you leave to deal with any issues of concern.
6. Propose the notion of separate vacations.

# GO FOR THE FUNNY BONE, NOT THE JUGULAR

Humor is a fabulous multi-purpose tool. When used properly, it can save face, save the day, and save your hide. I can't sit here and tell you how to be funny, how to slice through tension with a razor-sharp wit, or how to illuminate an issue with whimsical irony. What I can say is this: Humor works.

Make it work for you. When confronted with a difficult parent-raising challenge, try putting on a character. Play a role: be an astronaut, an alien, a witch, a judge, an infant, an athlete, a movie star, a police officer, a little kid. Be your mother, be your father (but don't be too accurate or the joke may be on you). Put on a funny voice, wear a costume, use props. Enlist the help of siblings in supporting roles.

You're banking on the possibility that a novel and humorous approach to an old issue will break through long-standing resistance. Your parents' admiration for your wit, perseverance, and unmitigated gall will, with any luck, endear you to them. If the gods of humor are on your side, this could change a "no" to a "maybe," and a "maybe" to a "yes."

CAUTION: Sarcasm is generally not funny. Be careful with it. Never direct it towards your parents (at least not under the category of humor. Perhaps it would belong under death-defying stunts). If you do use sarcasm, be sure it's clear that it's part of your role, and not part of a critique of your parents.

# GET PROFESSIONAL HELP

While seeing a counselor can be as expensive nowadays as getting your hair cut, I'll assume that one way or another you have access to someone, whether it's a school counselor, a community social worker, a psychologist, or a psychiatrist.

There are two reasons for you to see a mental health professional:

1. Because you want to talk with one, and/or
2. Because you want to get your parents to talk with one.

The first reason speaks for itself. There are times when problems are too much for one person to handle. You need advice, privacy, distance; you need someone who will listen, who doesn't have an ax to grind. Seeing a counselor can be a tremendous help. It can be an oasis of support and calm that will let you grab hold, figure things out, get back on an even keel. If your parents won't support your getting professional help, either financially or emotionally, then do it on your own. Look in the phone book under "Mental Health Services" or ask a trusted friend, teacher, coach, or doctor to help you find someone who will see you for little or no money.

The second reason for seeing a counselor—to get your parents to talk to one—is a little trickier but well worth the effort. You may feel that your parents are truly and objectively unreasonable, mistrustful, cruel, or unfair. If they are all those things, chances are slim that they would admit to it, and slimmer still that they would seek professional help. But chances are good that they've labeled you as the problem. GREAT!! If they think you're the

problem, they're playing right into your hands. Since you're the problem, ask them if you can get help—to work on some of your problems. With any luck, they'll agree. So far, so good.

Once you start seeing someone, he or she will want (especially if you favor it) to talk to your parents—after all, they're so close to all of your problems. That's the whole point of this strategy. You can use the fact that you've been identified as the problem as a means of getting your parents into a therapeutic situation. While this may not get them into weekly sessions for the next two years, it will provide an opportunity for your counselor, under the cover of seeing you, to meet with your parents. He or she can then say things to them that you never could; who knows what doors could open? Everyone will benefit. And if your parents don't open their minds or follow through, you've lost nothing. You still have your own supportive therapist. If you feel a bit anxious about seeing someone, that's only natural. But don't worry, there's nothing to be a-Freud of.

# P·RAISING PARENTS

Note the similarities between "raise" and "praise." This is no coincidence. It has long been recognized that one of the best ways to raise a parent is to praise a parent.

Praise is an effective tool in bringing up parents for three reasons:

1.  You will boost your parents' self-esteem. They will be more confident as parents and, as we all know, a confident parent is a happy parent. A happy parent is more apt to spread good cheer in the children's direction.

2.  Praise is a form of positive reinforcement for appropriate behavior. Studies involving rats, mice, dogs, and parents have all demonstrated that the best way to get an animal to repeat a behavior is to give a reward immediately after the desired behavior. When your parents do something you like, let them know right away by your praise. They'll be much more likely to repeat the action.

3. People notice what you do, not what you say. Actions count louder than words. Your praise models the attitude you'd like your parents to develop towards you. Show them how good it feels to be praised. The more you praise them, the more likely they will be to learn the art themselves and use it on your behalf.

# WRITE A NOTE

You can't go wrong with this indispensable instrument of explanation, adulation, or apology. It's the ultimate in intimate: special delivery with T.L.C. People l-u-v-v-v to get letters and this is express mail sealed with a kiss.

Why does note-writing work so well?

1. Parents adore getting notes from their kids. It hits them in a soft spot. A note means you care. A note means you're communicating (and you know how parents love to be communicated to). A note causes a lump in the throat of the parent who receives it; it's a reminder of how little baby has grown—why, just yesterday you were in your didies and booties, and now just look at you, pen in hand, scrawling a heartfelt message for their eyes only.

2. A note, like a diamond, is forever. While the spoken word may vanish in a spray of saliva, the written word lives on. It has power and presence unmatched by the mere exercise of vocal chords. Remember, the pen is mightier than the chord.

3. A note provides time, privacy, and distance for both sender and receiver. In the heat of an argument, people say things they don't mean and mean things they don't say. With a note, you can take the time to say exactly what you feel. You can consider your viewpoint, motives, emotions, and goals carefully. You can control your presentation without risk of unexpected flies in the ointment.

4. A note demands (in a polite way) a response from the receiver. The response usually reflects the level of caring and thoughtfulness contained in the original communication. Again, more power to you. You decide the plane on which this scene is acted out.

# When to Write a Note

- Write a note when you are too afraid, upset, embarrassed, apologetic, furious, and/or confused to speak your mind.
- Write a note when you want to use the power of the pen to give the greatest weight to what it is you have to say.

There are far too many types of notes to cover them all here. There are explaining notes, questioning notes, and apologizing notes. There are praising notes, loving notes, and thanking notes. There are reminding notes, forgiving notes, and pleading notes.

**Dear Dad,**

**I just wanted to say that I think you're the greatest!!!!!!! It meant a lot to me that you didn't chew me out in front of my friends even tho I know you were so mad. Thanks for waiting until we got home. I did want to explain exactly how come it was that I yelled like Tarzan during the second act....**

Corny? Of course. But parents love corn. So give 'em corn and they'll love you. 'Ears to corn!

- Don't forget the "I'm so sorry, Uncle Albert" type of note. Use it for apologies, explanations, for "...upon further reflection, I have come to see the error of my ways...."

- Use a note to explain clearly and respectfully why you believe your parents are wrong or unjust. (Remember the importance of style.)

- If you've just had a big fight, wait for the smoke to clear. Once your parents have retreated to their bunkers and you to your bunk, slip a note under their door. Sooner or later, you'll be:

  —hugged and loved for your apology

  —hugged and loved for your gracious praise

  —hugged and loved for your forgiving spirit

  —hugged and loved for your insightful explanation

  —hugged and loved for caring enough to send the very best—yourself.

Now you know why kids are required to take English composition in school. So they can be hugged and loved for writing notes.

NOTE: If you can't stand being hugged and loved by your parents, send 'em a note to that effect.

# CHOOSING PARENTS WITH CARE

Most of us do not have this opportunity. But you, oh lucky one, do. Make the most of it. By this time in your life, you've had ample opportunities to study your parents. With your recently acquired intelligence-gathering skills (see Chapter 2), you can expand your knowledge of these unique creatures even more. Armed with this information, you should be able to choose the best parent to approach in any given situation.

Whether you're looking for a handout, an exception to the rule, a "yes," a reprieve, or a good piece of advice, figure out which parent is your best bet. Don't just go to whomever happens to be handy. There's nothing dishonest about approaching the parent that you think offers the best chance for success. If you

wanted flowers, you wouldn't go to the butcher, would you? And if you wanted to swim, you wouldn't go to the skating rink. So why go to your mom if you know you'll have a better chance of getting what you want from your dad?

There's one condition, though. You're only entitled to one shot. You can't ask one parent, and then if you get an answer you don't like, go to the other parent. Going to one parent after being turned down by the other has the effect of acting as if the first parent doesn't exist. Parents don't like that. You'll either lose some trust and good will, or you'll create a fight between your parents and they'll both be upset with you. Recognizing that many of you will be unwilling to give up this behavior (after all, it does sometimes work), how about a compromise?

> *Your best friend, Susie, has invited you for a sleepover. You ask your dad. He says, "No."*

> *When you go to your mom for a second opinion, you're up-front about the fact that you already asked your father.*

> *"Mom, I asked Dad if I could sleep over at Susie's tonight and he said no. How do you feel about it? There's no school tomorrow."*

> *"I don't know. I don't mind if you sleep over. Why don't you tell your father it's okay with me and ask him if there was a particular reason he didn't want you to go."*

> *"Do you think you could ask him?"*

> *"No. It would be better if you did."*

With any luck, you'll work things out with your dad. You'll get to go to Susie's, your dad won't feel you pulled a fast one, your mom is saved from a potential argument with your father, and you are not saddled with the image of a sneaky, two-timing operator. O happy day! Have a good time at Susie's.

# PLEASE

Contrary to popular opinion, the word "please" was never invented for the benefit of adults. Its function has always been to give teenagers a boost in getting what they want. This is your word. Use it in any of its varieties. It's up to you to match form to function.

For maximum mileage, you can choose "please," "pleeze," "puh-leeeeze," or "PLEASE!!!" Also consider "p-p-p-please," "pretty please," or "pretty please" with one of its many toppings, such as "pretty-please-with-a-cherry-on-top" or "pretty-please-with-a-hot-fudge-sundae."

Once you've determined the best word form, find a suitable posture or gesture for reinforcement. Hands clasped in prayerful beseechment have been known to turn around even the most hardened "NO!" Similar success has been reported by those who drop to the knees and aim a doleful stare in the direction of the parent target while whispering the soft incantation of a "pretty-please-with-honey."

There's a plea in every please. That's why it works and why you can't go wrong with this handy-dandy helper-outer. Keep in mind the motto of the Please Academy:

- Forget "please" and it will be the bane of your existence.
- Remember "please" and it will be the gain of your existence.

# THANK YOU

Most effective when it's least expected. Of course, you'll say "thank you" when your parents honor your "please" pleas, or when you're overflowing with joyous gratitude at the sight of a birthday present.

The time to really milk every ounce of benefit from a "thank you" is when your parents have just done something that they consider to be an everyday responsibility of parenthood: giving you a ride, helping with homework, responding to a request for advice, putting dinner on the table. The fact that you say "thank you" at times like these will carry the words straight to that happy, loving spot in their heart. They will fill with warmth and kindness as they realize that you *do* appreciate the little things they do every day, that you don't take them for granted. Rarely can so much be gained from so little. How can you pass up this easy-street opportunity?

You're welcome.

# Chapter 4

# TAKING CHARGE OF THE FIGHT BRIGADE:

## STRATEGIES FOR BETTER RELATIONSHIPS

# IT'S NOT WHAT YOU SAY, IT'S HOW YOU SAY IT

This is often what parents mean when they don't like your "attitude." What a pity if this is an issue in your house! You see, it's all so unnecessary, because it's possible for you to say and do just about anything you want *if you know how.* There's tremendous power in that idea. Power that you can put to work for yourself at home, with your friends, and when you're out and about in what is commonly called the Real World.

What we're talking about here is *style*—how you come across to other people. People react to style, not substance. Often it's not *what* you say, it's *how* you say it. In many ways, that's a shame. It allows some people to get away with murder while others land in a pile of trouble because of a slip of the tongue or emotion. But that's how it is.

Have you ever known someone who says the most outrageous things? Someone who insults, teases, and sneers at people, and they eat it right up? "Oh," they say, "isn't he just something else? He is s-o-o-o outrageous! Don't you just love it?"

Assuming this person isn't 7'6" and 300 pounds, he gets away with it because there is something in his style, something in how he says what he says that makes it acceptable, if not downright delightful, to those who hear it. It might be a twinkle in his eye, a brilliance in his wit, a wink, a touch, a self-mocking posture. It might be the care with which he chooses his audience and target, but whatever the reason, it works for him. If another person made identical comments, he'd get himself slugged. Same words, different style.

Your style is a sometimes studied, sometimes unconscious mix of many factors. When communicating, the way you are received is affected by many elements:

- Your body. (Are you tensed up, turned away, slouching, pointing a finger, shaking a fist?)
- Your timing. (Are you speaking fast? Slowly? What moment did you choose for your communication? How do you pause, space your words?)

- Your facial expression. (Are you smiling? Squinting? Raising eyebrows? Gritting teeth?)
- Your tone of voice. (Are you shouting? Whispering? Sneering? Whining?)
- Your choice of words. (Are they biting? Accusative? Pretentious? Emotionally laden? Ambiguous?)

How you say what you say also reflects the situation, the context. What just happened? Who's around? What moods are people in? What's going to happen next?

Your style changes if you're talking to a friend, a baby, a parent, a teacher, a stranger. It changes if you know the person you're talking to is depressed, preoccupied, angry, impatient, ecstatic. You choose words to match mood, personality, your history with the listener.

There's nothing phony about this; there's no single you. Why shouldn't you allow the many parts of yourself to find expression? All the world's a stage, and as you act out your life, you can have a wonderful time playing the instrument of your person with skill and sensitivity as you relate to ever-changing people, places, and purposes. The more control you exert over the elements of your style, the more power you'll have to be effective and assertive, to get what you want, to grow, to become intimate with people, and to bring your parents up to be more sensitive and supportive. This power will help you prevent those problems that occur simply because you come across differently than you intended, because your style offended.

Sarcasm, accentuation, and all the elements of your style can give many different meanings to the same words.

- "I *don't* believe you!" (said to a friend who swears she didn't tell your boyfriend one of your secrets).
- "I don't buh-*leeve* you!" (said to a friend who just streaked naked in front of the stage during assembly).

You can see how the same words carry many different meanings because of style and context. A comment that would provoke laughter if made by a four-year-old could provoke stunned silence if made by a 14-year-old.

With the infinite variety of the English language, why is it that most parents and kids latch onto the most destructive, self-defeating styles for talking to one another? Why do parents choose words, expressions, and voice tones

that come across as an attack?  Why is it that their words appear to make things worse instead of better, to confuse rather than clarify?  Why can't parents and kids talk to each other?

Because they don't know how.  Parents repeat what they heard from their parents, kids repeat what they hear from their parents, and another negative cycle is established.  Cycles, remember?  Destructive patterns of stuck behavior.  Patterns that won't change unless you take action.  And act you must.  The reason is simple: to avoid all those problems that occur between parents and kids that are the result of poor communication, bad style.

Think of any communication as having two parts:

1.  The sending of a message, and
2.  The receiving of a message.

This holds true whether the message is spoken or unspoken; whether it is sent via words, facial expressions, gestures, touches, body positions, or a combination of these.  With parents and kids, something often gets in the way, communication is blocked, and problems multiply.  This can happen for many reasons:

- Vocabulary.  (Words can be misused or not understood.)
- Lack of attention, daydreaming, tuning the sender out.
- Mishearing.  (Thinking one thing was said when actually it was something else.)
- Being overloaded with emotion.
- Incorrect assumptions about the mood, feelings, experience, or motivation of the other person.
- A hidden agenda.
- Fear of revealing a true feeling or attitude.
- Speaking in such a way that the listener feels attacked, defensive, judged, ridiculed, preached to, analyzed.  (Sound familiar?  It should.  This is how your parents so often address you.  And perhaps you them.)
- Listening in such a way that the speaker feels ignored, trivialized, stereotyped, rejected.  (Bet this sounds familiar, too.)

It's useless to search for blame in faulty communications.  Sure, you could probably look at a single instance and say that the speaker wasn't clear, or the receiver wasn't paying attention, but communication always involves at

least two people. If a sender isn't clear, it then becomes the responsibility of the receiver to guide the communication to clarity. You'll suffer just as much from the consequences of poor communication whether it's your fault or the other person's. Whether you're speaking or listening, you have a responsibility to check the accuracy of the communication.

Since communication involves sending (speaking) and receiving (listening), if we look at new ways to send and receive messages we can avoid the obstacles to communication prevalent in so many families. It won't be easy, since the negative cycle of poor communication styles is deeply ingrained, but fear not, there are specific steps you can take to bring your parents up to be better communicators. You will need to model the behavior for them, and it may take some time before they pick it up; you know what slow learners adults can be. But your efforts will be rewarded.

Won't it be nice when your parents speak to you with respect, honesty, and sensitivity? Won't it be nice when they stop belittling, moralizing, and judging? Won't it be nice when you can cross off your list those problems that arise solely because of poor styles of communication?

## Mirror, Mirror Off the Wall: Active Listening at Work

Let's focus on getting your parents to listen to you without criticizing and attacking. In order to do this, you have to teach them to become Active Listeners. In order to do that, I have to show you how to become an Active Listener. You can then use the technique on your parents. They'll be so thrilled by your listening skills that they'll want to know how to do it themselves. They'll either pick it up on their own, or you can teach them. (Which is what you're after all along!)

Active Listening (or "reflective listening," as it's sometimes called) is a way of listening that:

- Encourages another person to talk,
- Makes the speaker feel understood, respected, and accepted,
- Checks the accuracy of the communication, and
- Minimizes chances for flare-ups and further problems.

The communication skills of Active Listening and "I-messages" (which you'll hear more about shortly) were developed by a number of therapists, prominent among them Rudolph Dreikurs and Dr. Thomas Gordon. These methods work; they're based on how people act and react. They're so simple to learn, yet few people use them. Be one of the few!

The key to Active Listening is *acceptance*. Active Listening is a way of showing that you understand and accept another person's feelings. This gets tricky, because feelings can cause a lot of trouble. Feelings can be hard to identify, hard to communicate, and risky to expose. Yet everyone has them and wants them to be heard and accepted.

Don't confuse acceptance with agreement. You don't have to agree with a feeling in order to accept it. You don't even have to believe the feeling is justified. You are simply granting your parents the right to have their own feelings.

Don't you hate it when they judge your feelings, when they act as if you don't have a right to your own feelings?

**"You shouldn't feel that way."**

**"How can you be so emotional?"**

You're not asking them to feel the same way you do, and you're not asking them to change how they feel. You're just saying, "Hey, this is who I am and how I feel. You don't have to feel this way or agree with my feeling, but can't you just accept the fact that this is how I do feel?"

The techniques of Active Listening are ways of saying:

**"I hear you."**

**"I understand your feeling."**

**"I accept the fact that that's how you feel."**

**"I accept your right to have those feelings."**

**"I may not like it, I may not want to hear it, I may not change my behavior because of it, but I accept you and your feeling."**

That's all people want. You'll be amazed at the change in your parents when you start to listen to them with the skills of an Active Listener. You'll be amazed how quickly you can defuse arguments, turn bad vibes into good ones, and build motivation in your folks to treat you the same way.

There are four specific techniques that make up Active Listening. The first three you probably know and use already.

1. ***Pay close attention.*** Show that you're tuned in, that you're really listening. Your silence, eye contact, and alert posture indicate your attentiveness. Together they say, "I care about what you're saying."

   You know this method, because you're already proficient with its opposite. When your parents are chewing you out, what do you do? You roll your eyes, you look anyplace but at them. You slouch, tap your foot, drum your fingers, doodle on paper. You shift position, you sigh, you do everything to communicate Total Lack of Attention. That's fine if your goal is to get your folks even madder, but it's disastrous if your goal is to reduce fighting.

2. ***Grunt and nod.*** Those occasional grunts, nods, "hmmms," "yeahs," and "uh-huhs" are excellent ways to indicate you're in full listening gear. (Remember, listening doesn't mean agreeing!)

3. **"...and then what happened?"** You can use short words and expressions to keep your folks talking and to show them they're being heard. Phrases like, "What then?" "Go on," "So...," "And...," "After that?" "Oh, wow," "Excellent!" "No kidding?" "Really?" "Like, cosmic," can all be used to good results.

4. **Reflect the feelings.** This is the most sophisticated Active Listening technique. The first three show that you're listening. This one shows that you're *understanding*. That's why it's so valuable and powerful.

   You're going to be a mirror. You're going to reflect your parents' feelings back to them. Not their words, but their feelings. This doesn't mean that you agree with what they say, it just means that you accept their feelings and grant them the right to have them. The mutual respect and affection created by this skill will avoid conflicts, encourage greater accuracy and honesty, and oil the squeaky wheel of your family's communication.

   When your parents make a statement, listen for the feeling behind it. Forget the words. They're just clues to the feeling. When you think you've identified the feeling, send it back to them. Be a mirror. You may be wrong, but that doesn't matter. If you are, they'll come back with a message of correction or further explanation.

Now that you know the basic techniques of Active Listening, let's watch them at work.

> *"Where on earth have you been? It's after midnight and you were supposed to be home over two hours ago!"*

What's the feeling? Anger? Sure, there's anger, but anger usually is a mask for a deeper feeling. You can be angry because you feel guilty or foolish, hurt or betrayed, impatient or ignored. Your parents are often angry with you, so you've got to figure out that deeper, hidden feeling for full Active Listening effectiveness. In the case of this parent, chances are good that the feeling of anger came about because of worry. Hidden in the message is:

> *"How could you do this to me? I've been worried sick about you, imagining that you were run over, mugged, kidnapped."*

Let's see how Active Listening would work in this situation.

*"Where on earth have you been? It's after midnight and you were supposed to be home over two hours ago!"*

*"You must have been really worried about me."*

*"I'll say I've been worried. I've been worried sick! What happened?"*

*"The Murphys got a flat on the turnpike and they didn't have a spare. We had to wait over an hour before a truck even came. I couldn't call, we were in the middle of nowhere. I can see why you were worried, but there wasn't anything I could think of to do."*

*"Well, at least you're back safe and sound. You look cold. Want some hot chocolate?"*

Well done! A blow-up was prevented by making the parent feel understood and accepted. You may think that the parent was silly to worry, or unjustified for jumping on the kid without even waiting for an explanation. And you may be right. But that's not the point. The point is that the parent was worried, and the fact that the kid recognized that worry and communicated acceptance is what avoided adding fuel to the fire.

Now watch what could have happened if the kid had responded to this attack in more typical fashion.

*"Where on earth have you been? It's after midnight and you were supposed to be home over two hours ago!"*

*"What are you yelling at me for? I didn't do anything."*

*"Don't talk back to me. You're two hours late. If this is the kind of responsibility you're going to show, you're grounded."*

*"You don't even know what happened. I could've been dead and all you talk about is grounding me. It wasn't my fault!"*

*"I don't care. If you can't be trusted to get home on time, you're not going to be allowed out."*

See what's happening? The parent is riled up with emotion. The feelings remain unidentified and have no place to go except towards the kid. The kid feels unjustly attacked (rightly so, in my opinion) and strikes back. Parent and

kid may argue all night about responsibility, restrictions, and trust without the explanation for the incident ever surfacing. The fact that the kid is blameless has nothing to do with the outcome.

NOTE: Right and wrong often have little to do with the course of an argument or the solution of a problem. That's because feelings get in the way of reason. Acceptance of feelings, however, has everything to do with improving relationships and minimizing conflict.

Watch Active Listening at work in another situation.

> *"Lucy! I thought I asked you kids to clean up the family room. Company's coming in two hours. Do I have to do everything around here? Can't I get any cooperation? There isn't one thing I won't do for you, and all I ask is for a little help now and then."*

Here's how most kids would respond to this attack.

> *Kid A: "Just a minute." (Ignores mom as if she didn't exist. Look out!)*

> *Kid B: "Well, I have a lot of things to do, too, you know." (Defensive, snippy. Spells trouble.)*

> *Kid C: "Why don't you ask Jamie? He never does anything around here." (Uh-oh. Run for cover.)*

Does Lucy take the bait or use Active Listening?

> *"I guess you feel like everything falls to you." (Whew. She used Active Listening.)*

> *"I certainly do and I'm tired of it. I only have one pair of hands, you know."*

> *"You must feel let down when we don't come through."*

> *"Yes, I do. But I'd still appreciate it if you could pitch in right now and give me a hand."*

> *"Okay. Jamie, Lisa! Mom needs our help right now. Come on down."*

Every time her mother said something, Lucy listened carefully and identified the feeling. Instead of becoming defensive, she reflected her mother's feelings back to her. Each time this happened, Mom became less upset. There were no miracles involved; Mom just felt understood and accepted as a person. That made all the difference in the world.

Sometimes, though, an incident can trigger many different feelings. How do you know which feelings are underneath a message? This is where intelligence-gathering comes in. You've got to be enough of a spy to make educated guesses as to the feelings in force. Look for clues. The more you know about your parents as people, and especially about any pressures they may be under, the better you can Actively Listen and increase the accuracy of your feedback.

You don't have to give anything up to Actively Listen in this way. You keep your feelings and your integrity. You don't have to agree, you don't have to argue, you just have to say, "I hear how you feel." Why try to work through an argument by focusing on right and wrong? You know how hard it is to get people to change their minds. Work the argument through by Active Listening. It does wonders.

**It will take time and practice to master Active Listening skills. The next few pages contain seven sophisticated pointers for, cautions about, and criticisms of Active Listening. DO NOT READ THEM until you are ready to get the nitty-gritty of these techniques under your parent-raising belt.**

1. *Active Listening does not necessarily eliminate feelings.* If your parents feel disappointed or betrayed by something you've done, they're going to feel that way for a while. Active Listening won't make the feelings disappear. What it will do is keep the feelings from getting worse and the situation from mushrooming into a nuclear family blast.

2. *Active Listening works best when your parents are on your case, when they see your behavior as a source of trouble, when their needs aren't being met.* In other words, when they scold, yell, attack, and lecture. If your reaction lets them know that they've been heard, they may be perfectly agreeable to letting your behavior continue, leaving a choice up to you, or forgetting the whole thing. It's when they don't feel heard that they'll keep after you.

3. ***Active Listening is a great way to improve communication with anyone.*** There doesn't have to be a problem that involves you. Have you ever been with friends when they're upset and you don't know what to say or how to help? You feel like giving advice, consoling, saying "don't worry." But that's not necessarily what will help them. Reflect their feelings back to them—it will keep them talking, and you'll all feel better.

4. ***Identifying feelings is difficult to do.*** People learn to hide, discount, and ignore their feelings. Consequently, a lot of people end up unable to recognize feelings in themselves and others. They'll use the words, "I feel," when they really mean, "I think."

   *"How do you feel about the American invasion of the Galapagos Islands?"*

   *"Well, I feel that we should have done it a long time ago considering the strategic importance of tortoises to our economy."*

That's not a feeling. That's an opinion, a thought. A "feeling" response would have been:

   *"I feel proud that we've finally gone in there."*

   *"I feel afraid that we may get in deeper than imagined."*

   *"I feel ashamed that our country could have done something like that."*

5. ***You may be embarrassed and uncomfortable at first when you use Active Listening.*** That's quite natural. It takes time to get used to new skills. Think of your first time on skis, your first bike ride, your first kiss. For a while, you probably felt self-conscious, but the awkwardness soon disappeared, and these new activities became so much a part of you that you could do them with your eyes closed. (Especially kissing.) Just to help, though, here are some phrases that, when combined with a reflected feeling, make good Active Listening starters:

| The Starters | Fill in the Feeling |
|---|---|
| *"You must feel pretty...* | *...upset."*<br>*...irritated with me."*<br>*...furious."* |
| *"Sounds like...*<br>*"Seems as if...* | *...you feel disappointed that*<br>*I forgot."* |
| *"I bet...* | *...you hoped for more help*<br>*than you got."* |
| *"You mean...*<br>*"Are you saying that...*<br>*"Is it that...* | *...you're worried about my*<br>*being out alone?"* |

6. ***When not to use Active Listening.*** While there are times when Active Listening will save the day, there are other times when Active Listening would be silly. It's a tool to be used selectively.

   If your father yells from the den, "I'm freezing. Could someone please close the door?" he's not in need of having his feelings heard. He's in need of having the door shut. A response of, "Gee Dad, you must feel cold," will only result in an icy stare.

   *"Would you kids hurry up!?!? We're going to be late if we don't get a move on."*

   *"Why, father, you sound impatient and concerned about whether we'll miss the show."*

   Duh. Once again, this parent doesn't need Active Listening. This parent needs to see some kids moving their tails out the door.

7. ***Active Listening doesn't necessarily solve problems.*** Active Listening is a way to communicate that promotes respect, sanity, and calmness. Active Listening may solve a problem by making your parents feel understood and valued. But it's also possible that after you've listened, the problem will remain. Even if emotions have settled down, there

125

could still be a conflict of needs, a strong difference of opinion. If that's the case, you have at least two options at your disposal:

- Bring the issue up at a Problem-Solving Session (see Chapter 5).
- Ask your parents if they have any suggestions. Any of these lines could be used to open the door to a solution:

*"Do you have any thoughts about what we could do?"*

*"Maybe we could think of another way."*

*"Want to put our heads together and see if we can come up with a solution?"*

*"I had no idea you felt that way. Can you think of anything we could do to change that?"*

The most important thing to keep in mind is that you can't move to a problem-solving mode until the feelings have been heard and accepted. There's a lot of truth to the expression, "I'm so upset I can't think straight." Once you and your folks have calmed down, you'll all be able to think straight.

Active Listening is one way to break the cycle of negative communication in your family. It's a way to encourage your parents to be more honest, to let go of issues, to stop nagging. It will build mutual respect and affection. Instead of responding with stony silence or sullen back talk, you'll be responding with:

*"I hear what you're saying."*

*"I understand that this is how you feel."*

*"I accept your right to have feelings."*

By not reacting to your parents the way they react to you, you're taking the first (and hardest) step towards breaking this cycle. While your folks may still deny your feelings, preach, psychologize, judge, and attack for a while, soon you will have isolated them in those behaviors. They'll feel out of synch with the new way you treat them, and the good feelings they'll have from feeling accepted will make them turn around and, bit by bit, become more accepting of you.

# When It Pays to Be Self-Centered: You-Messages versus I-Messages

Remember the two parts of communication? Sending and receiving? Active Listening works when you're the receiver of a message, when someone else is telling you about a problem, a need of theirs that you're thwarting, or a conflict in which you're involved. Active Listening is a great way to get your parents to talk to you and to let go of troublesome feelings. It's a way of listening so people will talk.

But that's only half of the picture. What about when *you* have a problem? When you want to send a message? How can you talk when you want your parents to listen? How can you communicate without triggering an avalanche of hostility and counterattack from your parents?

To answer those questions, let's reverse the situation for a moment. In order to figure out what will work, let's identify what doesn't work. Chances are that what turns you off also turns your parents off. How do your parents talk to make you feel hurt and attacked? What do they say that makes you close your ears faster than hearing a jackhammer outside your bedroom window?

*"You never do what you're told."*

*"You ought to be more careful."*

*"You never think of anyone but yourself."*

*"You should try harder."*

*"Can't you be more responsible?"*

*"Can't you show a little consideration for others?"*

Makes your skin crawl, doesn't it? Now, how does it sound from your parents' point of view? What do they hear when you talk to them?

*"You never let me do anything."*

*"You don't understand."*

*"You have no right to stop me."*

*"You always take her side."*

**"You don't trust me."**

**"You always act as if you know everything."**

It's enough to make them want to exit, stage left.

What do all these phrases, yours and theirs, have in common? The word *you*. They are all You-messages. *You* did it. *You* didn't do it. It's *your* fault, *you're* to blame. You-messages attack, condemn, and hurt. You-messages are guaranteed to antagonize, offend, and block communication. You-messages invite argument, outrage, and name-calling. You-messages back people into corners.

The effect of You-messages has nothing to do with right or wrong, with whether the content of the statement is accurate or not. The statement may very well be true. But remember, we're talking about *style*, about *how* you say *what* you say.

You-messages are *bad style*. The style—not the words or ideas, but the style—creates emotions that block communication. The receiver of a You-message feels labeled, judged, put down. You-messages attack the person, not the action. You-messages cause trouble. You-messages are how many parents and kids talk to each other. Another destructive cycle has been established, and you must break it in order to bring up parents who will speak respectfully and lovingly.

How can you break this cycle? Let's go back to the way your folks talk to you.

**"You never do what you're told."**

Suppose that instead of attacking you, instead of taking the easy way out and laying this trip on your doorstep, your parents got in touch with their feelings. Suppose that instead of a You-message, they sent an I-message. Suppose that they said specifically *how they feel* about *your behavior* and *its consequences* for them.

What if, instead of "You never do what you're told" (which can't possibly be true anyway), they said:

**"When we ask to have something done and it doesn't get done, we feel ignored and hurt."**

Doesn't that go down a little easier? It's not an attack on your entire being, it's a description of a situation and how it makes your parents feel. Sure, there may be a little sting to it; sure, it's talking about you; sure, you may disagree with their position—but it's said in a style that's more respectful, less accusative. It's the sort of a statement that opens communication rather than closes it. If your parents speak to you with an I-message, you're less likely to fly off the handle. You're more likely to respond with an equal measure of thought and concern. You could Actively Listen.

*"You feel like I don't listen to you?"*

Perhaps there's a simple misunderstanding.

*"I'm sorry, I didn't mean to ignore you. I had no idea you wanted me to take the rubbish out right away."*

Maybe you did blow it. No big deal if you come back with:

*"Oh, no! I totally forgot. Honest. I'll do it right away and try to remember next time."*

As long as there are people, there will be problems. But if people can work them out with respect for each other's feelings and perspective, relationships will be strengthened and trust can grow. The trick, then, in bringing up parents who will be sensitive to your needs and feelings, is to communicate so that you'll be heard. You don't want them to shut their ears to you just because of how you express something, just because of your style.

To the extent that a You-message fails to be heard, an I-message succeeds. An I-message will be taken seriously and increase the chances for positive change, a meeting of the minds, or at least a respectful difference of opinion.

It's quite simple to construct I-messages. They are statements that announce how you feel about someone else's behavior, attitude, or position and its consequences for you.

- First, *describe* to your parents the behavior that disturbs you or interferes with your needs. Don't accuse, name-call, or attack. Just describe.

*"When I can't stay out after eleven o'clock on Saturday nights..."*

**129**

■ Second, state how the consequences of that behavior make you *feel*.

> *"...I feel embarrassed..."*

■ Third, describe the *consequences*.

> *"...because the kids at school are all going around saying I'm a baby."*

There's no guarantee that your parents will change your curfew, but the way you expressed yourself will cause them to take you seriously and talk about it. With any luck, you may work it out. Don't you think your parents will hear this type of communication more readily than, "You always treat me like a baby!"?

To Actively Listen, you have to guess how someone else feels. To construct an I-message, you only have to know how you feel. For once, you have to be *self*-centered.

You might have many feelings about a particular situation. This means that you could create many I-messages:

> *"When I can't stay out after eleven o'clock on Saturday night I feel hurt because it makes me think you don't trust me."*

> *"When I can't stay out after eleven o'clock on Saturday nights, I feel angry because Sean was able to stay out until one in the morning when he was my age."*

Like Active Listening, I-messages are a tool to be used selectively. The three parts of an I-message—the behavior, the feeling, and the consequences—can be spoken in any order. Sometimes there may only be two parts: a behavior and a consequence, or a feeling and a behavior.

Use I-messages when you have a problem, when someone else is interfering with your needs. Use them when you want to comment on someone's behavior in such a way that you'll be heard. When you own a feeling, when you say, "Hey, this is how I feel about a situation," your honesty, openness, and respect will be returned. You invite someone to say:

> *"Hmmm, I had no idea."*

Or:

*"What can we do to change that?"*

Or:

*"Here's how I feel."*

You haven't attacked, you've described. You haven't blamed, you've extended a part of yourself.

I don't mean to imply that all you have to do to make everything good and sweet and right in your family is to use Active Listening and I-messages. Obviously, it's not that simple. Feelings and problems run deep. You can Actively Listen all day and I-message all night and still not resolve a conflict. You may have to bring an issue to a Problem-Solving Session (see Chapter 5). You may have to change your behavior; your parents may have to change theirs. You may have to apologize; you may need time to heal a wound. But how can you solve a problem if you can't even talk about it?

What Active Listening and I-messages do is provide a framework of style to encourage talking and listening between you and your parents. Fill that framework with who you are, and you've got a winning combination.

As you identify and eliminate elements of bad style from your family relationships, communication, closeness, and good feeling will grow. Let's look at more ways to change how kids say what they say. After all, it's one of the keys to bringing up parents who will treat you with respect and understanding.

## Request, Don't Command

Whenever possible, put your commands in the form of requests. You're much more likely to get what you want. You can think of it as a command, your parents will hear it as a request, and everyone will be happy.

**Bad**

*"Dad, you gotta take me to soccer practice now."*

*"I don't gotta do anything. I'm busy. Why didn't you tell me about this before now?"*

**Better**

*"Dad, can you take me to soccer practice now?"*

*"Please."*

*"Please?"*

**Best**

*"Dad, can you please take me to soccer practice now?"*

*"Sure. Just a sec; let me finish this up."*

You're probably wondering, "Why should I have to ask permission every time I want to do something?" You shouldn't. And you don't. We're talking style here. This is the media age, remember? Think of the network news. Anyone can read the news, but television stations spend millions of dollars searching for that newscaster with the style that's going to capture viewers and increase ratings. You have to search for the style, the how you say what you say, that will increase your ratings with your parents.

You already know where the limits on your freedom are. Obviously, you're not going to ask permission to do those things you know you can just do. "Mom, can I take a shower" and "Dad, can I make a phone call" sound pretty silly coming from a 15-year-old. But for those times when you're in that gray area between what you know you can do and what you're not sure you can do, or when you're clearly blazing new trails of freedom and independence, you'd do best to err on the side of a request. When in doubt, check it out.

The best way to honor your repulsion for asking and your parents' for being told is to split the difference. Watch.

*"I'm going to the mall.*
(Command part)

*Okay?"*
(Request part)

*"I'm going to the mall.*
(Command part)

*Is that all right with you?"*
(Request part)

*"Unless you have any objections,*
(Request part)

*I'm going to the mall."*
(Command part)

Any statement or request can be placed on a continuum of style that extends from utter rudeness to sublime politeness. Your job is to choose a style that locates your remark someplace in-between, where you're neither barking self-centered orders nor mousing around like an obsequious teacher's pet.

Here are two examples where the same content is expressed in different styles. You'll probably be most comfortable (as will your parents) someplace in the middle. After all, excessive politeness can be a little sickening to you and suspicious to your parents.

*"Would you be so kind as to please pass the potatoes?"*

*"Could you please pass the potatoes?"*

*"Could you pass the potatoes?"*

*"Pass the potatoes."*

*"Potatoes."*

*"Gimme the #$@&%*#! potatoes."*

And:

*"Could I please have permission to go to the movies tonight?"*

*"Could I please go to the movies tonight?"*

*"Can I go to the movies tonight?"*

*"I'm going to the movies tonight, okay?"*

*"I'm going to the movies tonight."*

*"I'm going out."*

*"Bye."*

*(A slamming door.)*

The more you choose a style that recognizes the existence of your parents, the more you'll bring up parents who will respect your freedom. If you like the sounds of "Yes," "Why, certainly," "It's all right with me," and "Of course, dear," then get used to the sounds of "Is it okay?" "Can I?" "Do you mind?" and "May I, please?" These sounds are music to everybody's ears.

# Don't You Dare Threaten Me or I'll. . . .

Threats will backfire. Issuing a threat to your parents is like waving a red flag in front of a bull. No matter how bullheaded your folks are, a threat will only make things worse. It will shift the argument to a no-win power struggle, where both sides feel backed into a corner. Whatever chance you might have had to get what you want will evaporate.

You know how you hate threats from your parents.

*"If you don't clean up this mess, you're not going out tonight and that's final."*

*"One more word out of you and you'll be sent to your room."*

*"Either you act more responsibly or there'll be no skiing this winter."*

Unfortunately, parents use threats all the time. Sometimes they work because their kid is afraid, wants something badly, or even knows deep down that there is justification to the parents' position. But even if the threat works, damage is done to the relationship.

The chances of a threat aimed at your parents working for you are slim. This is because parents hold so many of the power cards. They have the power to carry out their threats. They can cut off money, services, privileges, freedom. It's not fair, but they can do it. And do do it.

But what can *you* threaten?

*"If you don't increase my allowance, I'll smash your computer."*

*"If I can't go to this concert, I'll tell the Perkinses what you said about them."*

Somehow it seems unlikely that these threats will carry much weight or endear you to your parents. In fact, they'll probably turn around and say:

*"Don't you threaten me, or you'll be sorry."*

Given the fact that most kids have very little power in the parent-child equation, what do they do? Being clever, kids figure out what their parents care about most. Their children. And what would hurt their parents most?

Harm to their children!  Once they've discovered their parents' weak spot, they know where to aim a threat.

*"If you don't let me...*

*"...I'll hold my breath." (Age four)*

*"...I won't eat." (Age six)*

*"...I won't ever talk to you again." (Age eight)*

*"...I'll skip school." (Age thirteen)*

*"...I won't do my homework." (Age fourteen)*

*"...I won't ever invite a friend over again." (Age fourteen and a half)*

*"...I'll quit school." (Ages fifteen to eighteen)*

*"...I'll leave home." (Ages sixteen to eighteen)*

*"...I'll move back into the house." (Ages twenty-two and up)*

The problem with these threats is that you end up the loser.  In order to harm your parents, you have to harm yourself.  These threats back you into a corner; either you eat crow and give up on your threat, or you follow through and end up hurting yourself.  Not much of a choice.

Sure, if you abandon your social life, refuse to leave your room, or flunk school on purpose, your parents will be upset.  But ultimately you're the one with no friends who has to go to summer school.  The whole point was to get back at your parents, but all you've done is get back at yourself.

In families without mutual respect and good communication, kids make threats because they have no other choice.  It is in their ability to hurt and be destructive that their greatest power—a negative power—exists.  Your power will increase in positive ways as you utilize the techniques presented in this book.  The need to resort to threats will disappear.  So stop using them.  Or else!

## Don't Call Your Father a Butthead

Or an idiot, jerk, tightwad, dictator, or #@!&#!!.  (Even though you may think it at times.)  Calling your parents names and heaping slurs upon their character can only create new arguments.

I'd be the first to admit that there could be a momentary satisfaction in hurling a well-deserved epithet in the direction of an offending parent. But the benefit will be extremely short-lived, perhaps lasting only as long as the second it takes for your parent's hand to find the side of your face. In the long run, the damage you do to your image, your relationship, and your cheek is what will last.

When you call your parents names, look at all the new issues you create. First, the validity of your claim: Is or isn't your parent that which you named? Then there's the issue of whether your First Amendment rights extend to put-downs, as well as the ramifications of whatever response your parents elect. From what started as a little skirmish, you've escalated to a full-fledged war. Whatever caused the name-calling in the first place remains unaddressed.

Let's go back to the beginning and see what other options exist.

Something has happened to make you feel that your father is a real pain in the lower posterior. This is what you'd like to say on an emotional level. But stylistically, you just can't come out and say it. You saw what happened when you tried that. The question becomes, how can you tell your father he's being a jerk without offending him?

First, you have to get in touch with your feelings. What was it he did or said? How did that make you feel? That's what you want to communicate. Instead of saying:

**"Dad, you're such a sleazebag, slimeball scuzzbucket,"**

try something like this:

**"Dad, I've had to come home at the same time for over three years. I'm so mad 'cause I don't feel it's fair. I am more responsible now than I was three years ago, and I should be able to have more free-dom. Can we talk about this?"**

Now at least you've got a fighting chance. If you can avoid name-calling, if you can uncover any hidden agendas, if you can stay calm and rational, you may get to the real issue, and that's halfway home when it comes to solving a conflict. If, after all this, you aren't making any progress and your father is acting like he did before, well, maybe you were right in the first place.

But you still can't call him a butthead.

# Bye Cycles:  How to Put an End to Stereotyping

One of the most annoying habits of the parent beast is stereotyping its off-spring—summing up an entire human being in one word or phrase.  Don't you just hate it when your parents say:

> *"You're such a crybaby."*
>
> *"What a sneak you are."*
>
> *"You're nothing but a spoiled brat."*
>
> *"You're a selfish, ungrateful child."*
>
> *"All you do is complain and whine."*
>
> *"You live in a dream world."*

You may, like everyone else, be sneaky or selfish on occasion.  You may even complain, pout, and whine.  But it is highly doubtful that your personality consists of no other traits.  Surely there are times when you're brave, considerate, generous, and tolerant.  (Even if not to your parents.)

137

Stereotyping is a dangerous practice for two reasons:

1. It causes hurt. No one likes to be accused of selfishness, brattiness, crybabyness, whiny-ness, or Loch Ness monster-ness.

2. It has a way of coming true by encouraging the behavior it labels.

The stereotyper (your parent) will tend to notice only that behavior which confirms his or her opinion and to ignore behavior that doesn't. The stereotypee (that's you), having already been labeled, might as well live up to the image. What have you got to lose? If your parents have decided that you're nothing but a complainer, you might as well complain.

Stereotyping works in the other direction, too. Kids define their parents, with the same disastrous results.

**"You're such a worrywart."**

**"You never let me do anything."**

**"You're just a mean bully who likes to order kids around."**

How do you break the cycle of stereotyping?

1. Set an example. Don't stereotype your parents. The last thing you'd want is if they *did* live up to your label.

2. When they stereotype you, let them know how it makes you feel: hurt, hopeless, attacked, like giving up since their minds are already closed. Ask them if they could just comment on your actions without labeling your entire being.

3. Keep records that you can use to disprove the label. While this may seem silly and self-conscious, it'll get your message across. Your parents are sure to realize how much their stereotyping bothers you if the next time they call you a selfish, spoiled brat, you respond:

**"You know, ever since you started calling me a spoiled brat, I decided to keep notes to see if that's really true. I thought you'd be interested to hear things I do that aren't selfish...."**

Then tell them your list. Be calm about it. You don't want them to get all defensive, as if you're being disrespectful by challenging their opinion. (You just can't be too careful with parents—they can be s-o-o-o sensitive.)

# STOP! IN THE NAME OF LOVE

## Speech of the Devils: All-Time-Champion-Designed-to-Drive-Any-Healthy-Kid-up-the-Wall-Parent-Expressions!!

### "Because I Said So."

If you got a buck every time your parents flaunted this self-serving phrase, you'd be retired by now. This insulting figure of speech comes in four varieties, but, like a skunk, no matter how you dress it up, it still stinks.

The expression is invariably triggered by the inquiry, "Why not?"

*"Can I get my own phone?"*

*"No."*

*"Why not?" (Look out! Here it comes!)*

*"Because."*

*"Because why?"*

*"Because I said so."*

*"But I don't see why. I'll pay for it."*

*"Because I'm your mother and I said so, that's why."*

*"But why not? It won't cost you a cent! I said I'd pay for it. Why can't I get one?"*

*"Because I'm your mother and I said so and that's final!"*

You can plainly see how this mother escalated the definitiveness of her response by going sequentially through all four versions of the expression. Let's look a little more closely at this fearsome gang of four.

139

1. **"Because."** This is the least offensive version because it makes it sound as though you are the victim of some cosmic power greater than you or your parents. How can you fight the cosmos?

2. **"Because I said so."** This suggests the possibility that your parent is acting as an agent for said cosmic force and as such might be open to persuasion. Don't believe it!

3. **"Because I'm your mother/father and I said so."** This variation not only incorporates the content of the above two but throws in a reminder of your lowly status in the parent/child relationship. You're losing ground fast.

4. **"Because I'm your mother/father and I said so and that's final!"** This one pulls out all the stops. You're fighting mother, father, God, country, and the tide of the universe. Not a chance. Forget it.

We've got a tricky situation here. The fact that your parents have used a "because-I-said-so" response suggests that they are already either a) hassled or b) threatened. To pursue your quest for an explanation at this moment is likely to lead nowhere or to provoke your parents' second line of defense:

**"We don't owe you an explanation. You'll do as you're told."**

There are two things you can do to stamp out the use of these exasperating "becauses":

1. Utilize the strategies of this book as consistently as you can. "Because I said so" is a disrespectful remark. It dismisses you as a person, and it says that you have no right to know the reasoning behind a decision that affects your life. The whole point of this book is to increase the communication and shared decision-making in your family and to bring up parents who will respect you enough to explain their feelings and thinking. As time allows you to change your parents' attitudes, it will become increasingly unlikely that they will address you in such a demeaning manner.

2. Go up to the offending parent sometime after the episode has occurred. Choose a calm, untroubled opportunity when you're feeling cheerful and secure. (Oh, come on, that's got to happen once in a while.) You want to avoid threatening your parent. Try something like this:

*"Say, Mom? Remember the other day when I asked if I could have a phone and you said no?"*

*"Hmmm?" (Be careful. Mom is already tensing up.)*

*"I'm not asking you to change your mind or anything. I just wondered if you could explain what your reasons were. I mean, I was really surprised when you said no and I thought maybe if I could learn why you said no I'd understand your reasons and feel better about it."*

If you choose your moment well and come across in a friendly, natural way, you should get the explanation you desire. Listen carefully. After you know why your mom said "no," you may be able to come up with some ideas to overcome her objections. Whatever you do, don't attempt to challenge her reasoning now. Don't argue. Just gather your intelligence, thank her, and go.

You wouldn't want her to feel tricked. A big argument at this point would make her unwilling to give you an explanation in the future. She'd have grounds to say, "If I told you why, you'd only argue with me."

What you want to do is leave graciously, sending a little gratitude in your mom's direction for taking the time to explain her decision. Her reasoning may make sense to you and cause you to drop the whole thing. Or, if the objections she has are specific ones that you believe could be overcome, think up a proposal and bring it to a Problem-Solving Session (see Chapter 5).

Remember, the style you use must be one that communicates your acceptance of your parents' right to have feelings and opinions on these matters, even if you don't agree. Use Active Listening and I-messages to keep everything under control. But whatever you do, don't attack your parents when they make their explanation.

*"Why not?"*

Because I said so!

## "You Have No Respect for Authority."

Why should you? So much of the authority you're supposed to respect doesn't respect you! It is authority based upon fear and intimidation, authority designed to maintain the status quo, to keep you in your place and out of the way, where you won't be able to challenge it.

Of course you have no respect for that kind of authority. Neither would your parents, which is why it's so maddening when they utter this remark. It's too pat, too simplistic; it insults your sense of justice. If authority, in and of itself, should command respect, regardless of the values and behaviors associated with it, I guess the Founding Fathers who launched the American Revolution against tyranny had no respect for authority. And what about when Gandhi held fast to his position? He didn't exactly bow down to the powers that be'd.

You *do* respect authority. Next time your folks throw this line in your direction, tell them that. Tell them you respect authority that is fair and equal in application. Tell them you respect authority that preserves individual rights, that is based on concern and compassion, democracy and representation, fairness and dignity. Tell them. They may consider your remarks further evidence of your disrespect for authority. But, hey, Rome wasn't built in a day.

## "When I Was Your Age...."

You mean, like when dinosaurs roamed the land? Why does this expression produce yawns and rolled eyeballs? Why does terminal boredom descend upon even the most energetic teenager unfortunate enough to hear its utterance? For four good reasons:

1. The remark often introduces a LECTURE. We know what happens when kids realize they're about to receive a lecture from their parents. ZZZZZZzzzzzzzz.

2. The remark often accompanies an analysis, judgment, or put-down.

   *"When I was your age, I took pride in how I looked."* (*Back then, you had looks to be proud of.*)

   *"When I was your age, kids respected their elders."* (*Back then, elders were worthy of respect.*)

   *"When I was your age, I knew the value of a dollar."* (*Back then, a dollar had value.*)

3. The remark often is the lead-in to a completely irrelevant statement.

   *"When I was your age, I didn't spend all my time hanging out at the shopping mall."* (*That's because you grew up in the country, Dad.*)

4.  Finally, the remark is often the preface to sheer fantasy.

    *"When I was your age, I spent six hours a night doing my home-work."* *(Then how come Grandma says you never studied and flunked eighth grade?)*

    *"When I was your age, I didn't resent helping around the house."* *(That's because you grew up with a nanny, three maids, a gardener, cook, and butler.)*

Maddening, isn't it? It's hard to break parents of this habit. One way to at least reduce the number of times your folks lay this dreary line on you is to get there ahead of them. Gather intelligence. Ask your parents about their childhoods, families, school experiences, adolescent feelings, and social lives. The more you can satisfy their urge to talk about life "when I was your age," the less inclined they'll be to spring the line on you at an unguarded moment. If they're not trying to make a point with their reminiscence, the information is more likely to be honest and therefore valuable to you. They'll be flattered, you'll uncover nuggets of intelligence which will be helpful in other situations, and what would otherwise have been a losing proposition for all turns into a winning exchange of ideas and familial friendship.

## "Someday You'll Thank Us for This."

Yeah, right. And someday the cow will jump over the moon, your parents will stop telling you to be careful, and Birnham Wood will come to Dunsinane. "Someday you'll thank us for this" is enough to make any teenager's skin crawl and blood curdle. Talk about adding insult to injury! Twisting the knife! What an obnoxious expression. But wait—that's not all. There's another phrase equally odious in impact which can be (and is) used interchangeably:

## "It's for Your Own Good."

Both this phrase and the revolting "Someday..." are delivered by parents after inflicting a disappointment of epic proportions upon you. Instead of softening the blow, this preachy preposterousness only makes it a million and three times worse. Watch.

**143**

*Your parents have just said that they won't let you go to a rap con-cert at the Coliseum. You've already told your friends, "No prob-lem, of course I can go."*

*"Honey," they explain, with understanding oozing from their parental pores, "it's not that we don't trust you or want to make you unhappy. It's just that the Coliseum is a long drive from here and we're worried about your staying out so late and all the drugs and violence at these concerts. We know you don't agree but it's for your own good."*

How sitting at home on Friday night while all your friends are at the concert is "for your own good" is beyond even your keen powers of deduction. That's the last thing you want to hear. What you really want to hear is:

*"We know we're being cruel and unfair and treating you like a baby, and this is going to make you a laughingstock in front of your friends and you'll never be able to live it down. You have every reason to hate us and call us the worst parents in the world."*

There, feel better? Anything but the double whammy. The "no" is bad enough without the expectation that their action deserves your thanks and approval. For crying out loud (which is exactly what you feel like doing), if you've been stripped of your dignity, can't you at least be left with your misery?

Parents who utter these pompous remarks are really pushing their luck. Next time it happens to you, try one of these two ideas:

1. Ignore it. After all, if your parents are capable of making such a terri-ble decision in the first place, it only stands to reason that they would follow it up with a terrible remark. So what else is new? You should be used to it by now. Ignore to your heart's content, disappear into a deep meditation if necessary, and renew your commitment to carry out the strategies of this book so that in time, your parents will grow out of this infantile attitude.

2. Tell them, in your own words:

   *"I wish you wouldn't say that. If I can't go, I should at least be entitled to my feelings of anger!"*

# "We'll See."

*"Mom, can I go to the movies tonight?"*

*"We'll see."*

*"Dad, can you go with me Saturday to get my cassette player fixed?"*

*"We'll see."*

*"Can I...?"* *We'll see.*

*"Could you...?"* *We'll see.*

*"Is it all right if...?"* *We'll see.*

Who is this "we"? You ask a question of your mom, who's the only person in sight, and she answers, "We'll see." You're all alone with your dad in the car, pop a query, and he says, "We'll see." The other half of the "we" can't possibly be your other parent. If it were, your mom would say, "I'll have to ask your father," and your dad would reply, "Your mother and I will have to think about it."

It's definitely a mystery, this "we." No wonder searching for the "we" who will see becomes an eternal quest for teenagers. While you stalk this ubiquitous creature, it wouldn't be a bad idea to familiarize yourself with the many meanings of this phrase.

- **Meaning #1:** I'm Tired and Busy and Can't Deal with You Right Now. As in:

*"Can I invite some friends over for the night?"*

*"We'll see."*

- **Meaning #2:** The Answer Is No but I'm Not Going to Get into a Fight about It Now by Saying So. As in:

*"Is it all right if I go to the Pearsons' cabin at the lake with Janie and her older sister this weekend?"*

*"We'll see."*

■ **Meaning #3:** It All Depends on Your Behavior between Now and Then. How Good Are You Going to Be?  As in:

*"Can I have a Walkman for my birthday?"*

*"We'll see."*

■ **Meaning #4:** You've Stumbled on a Secret and I'm Not Going to Tell You.  As in:

*"Can I have a Walkman for my birthday?"*

*"We'll see."*

Last but not least comes the only acceptable use of the phrase as far as you're concerned:

■ **Meaning #5:** I Bet You're Expecting Me to Say No but Believe It or Not, There Is a Chance I'll Actually Say Yes.  As in:

*"Can I have a Walkman for my birthday?"*

*"We'll see."*

What should you do when your parents say, "We'll see"?  Remain calm, tolerant, and philosophical.  You are witnessing an innate behavior of the parent species.  (Quite similar to your use of the term, "Nothin'," as a retort to any number of weary queries.)  While it may be impossible to wean your folks from this habit, here are some suggestions for trying:

■ If you think your parent intends Meaning #1, you can say, "You seem busy now. I'll ask you later." (Better yet, help out and then pop the question again.  You may increase the yes probability quotient.)

■ If you suspect that Meaning #2 is afoot, you might as well get it over with by saying, "If the answer's no, I'd rather you just say so now and that way I won't get my hopes raised and dashed and my heart broken into a million pieces beyond despair and repair when you finally do say no."  That should bring the question to a head.

■ For Meaning #3, the choice is easy:  Be as good as you possibly can, and after any particularly good goodness on your part, drop a hint such as, "Say, Mom, have you ever listened to one of those headset stereos?" or "Boy, what I wouldn't give for a Walkman."

- For Meaning #4, just shut up and keep your fingers crossed.
- Finally, if you think your parent intends Meaning #5, immediately drop to your knees, assume a posture that is reverent if not downright fawning, and begin to chant:

*"Please, puh-leeeze, pretty please, if you say yes I'll be your friend for life, no, for life and two reincarnations, I'll even clean my room, please? Please?"*

# Out of the Mouths of Babes: Things Kids Say that Are Guaranteed to Make Their Parents See Red!!

- Not so you can *use* them; so you can *avoid* them.
- If you could only keep your mouth shut, you wouldn't always get in so much trouble!

## "You Can't Tell Me What To Do!"

Of course they can. Whether you do what they tell you or not is another matter. The problem with this expression is that it instantly changes any argument into a power struggle between you and your parents. Once this happens, you're all in big trouble, since your parents will never admit that they can't tell you what to do and you'll never admit that they can. So you'll have a big argument over their right to tell you what to do, which isn't even the issue. Unless you stuff socks in their mouths, they can always tell you what to do. What you really want to say is...

## "You Can't Make Me!"

That's more like it. If you're going to have a knock-down, drag-out power struggle, at least let it be over the correct issue: whether they can make you do that which they've told you to do, which you've told them they can't tell you to do in the first place. However, in spite of your instructions, they *have* told you what to do, and suddenly you're engaged in this dazzling dialogue:

*"I won't do it."*

*"Yes you will."*

*"Oh no I won't."*

*"Oh yes you will."*

*"Oh no I won't."*

*"Oh yes you will!"*

*"You can't make me!"*

*"We'll see about that!"*

The battle lines are drawn. The stakes increase. The war escalates. First, the light artillery:

*"There'll be no TV for a week."*

*"You can't make me."*

*"And you're not going to the game Friday."*

*"You can't make me."*

Your parents bring in reinforcements:

*"You better watch it or you'll be grounded for a month."*

*"I don't care, you never let me do anything anyway."*

*"If you're not careful, young man, you can forget about going away to camp this summer."*

You call their bluff:

*"You'd never do that. You wouldn't want me around all summer and you know it."*

Heavy armaments this time:

*"Don't be disrespectful." (A line often used by parents when their kids have hit upon the truth.) "You're grounded for an entire month, starting today. You're to come straight home from school. No TV, no friends over, no telephone."*

*"You can't make me."*

They know they can't make you. You're no longer four years old. The fact that it gets harder and harder for them to make you do the things they wish and prevent you from doing the things they don't wish is the key to one of the great parent-teenager power struggles. Which is exactly why you have to avoid using this expression. Power is at the heart of breaking away; as your power increases, your parents' power decreases. You can't attack the issue head-on. It's a no-win trap with each of you locked into a position.

Look at it this way. If you came across a garage full of raw sewage and skunk purée, would you avoid it? Of course you would. And what if you saw a pond full of piranhas on steroids? Would you dive in? Absolutely not. So why would you walk blindly into an abyss of confrontation that guarantees only that you will fall from your parents' graces?

The better you can avoid getting locked into a position, the better you can bring up parents who won't lock themselves or you into one. Instead of getting backed into opposite corners, meet in the middle, where a solution will be found. Your honor as a badge-carrying adolescent will not be diminished.

## "I Didn't Ask to Be Born, You Know."

Given our current knowledge of these matters, you do have a point. But just what is your point? This sort of discussion would have been better taken up in the womb. It all seems a bit moot now, and bringing it up at this time will only feed your parents' impression that you are immature and illogical, which is the last thing you need. Don't give them this type of ammunition. It can only hurt your cause.

## "Jimmy's Mother Lets Him Do It."

This expression provokes a reaction in your parents similar to yours when they say, "Finish your dinner. Children are starving in India." Yawn. Big so what. Of course, you care that children are starving in India and Pakistan and Africa and China and (though some don't believe it) in America. But what on earth does that have to do with finishing your dinner? It's not as if you can wrap up your mashed potatoes and Federal Express them to Calcutta. Whether you finish dinner or not isn't going to make one linguine's difference to poor, starving children.

To your parents, the expression, "Jimmy's mother lets him do it," has the same degree of relevance: None. Jimmy's mother might as well be in India with the starving children for all that she matters to the issue at hand. Jimmy's mother has nothing to do with you, your mother, your father, your household, or your problem. Which is probably why your mom will respond to your line with:

**"Well, I'm not Jimmy's mother, and you're not Jimmy."**
**(Brilliant, Mom!)**

Look, the planet's already heating up. For goodness' sakes, don't put any more hot air into the atmosphere.

## "You Just Don't Understand."

The ultimate dismissal. You can wipe your parents off the map with this line. Usually uttered in despair, "You just don't understand" is designed to make parents feel two inches tall. Even that may be too good for them after what they did to you.

In fact, what did they do to merit this all-encompassing finale of a put-down? Chances are, they didn't take you seriously. They laughed at something important to you, they denied your right to have certain feelings. They used their standards to judge your world. As if how *they* feel is how *you* should feel, as if how a 40-year-old reacts is how a 14-year-old should react.

**"You're being silly."**

**"It's just a stage you're going through."**

**"When you're older, you'll laugh at this."**

**"It's only a dance."**

**"You'll have other boyfriends."**

They want you to have a perspective that makes no sense in terms of your life, years, and development. Exasperated, your only recourse (up to now) has been to close the conversation and send your folks packing with a well-aimed "You just don't understand." What more can be said after that?

The problem is, if they don't understand now, they're not going to understand later. Nothing will change unless you make it change. With the strategies in this book, you don't need to use this phrase anymore. Now you have methods for making them understand. Use them instead.

## "I Don't Care."

Oh, yes, you do, or you wouldn't have said you don't. What happened? Did your parents just lay a power trip on you? A threat? So you're trying to pull the rug out from under them by showing an I-Don't-Care-Big-Wow-If-You-Expect-to-Get-a-Rise-out-of-Me-Try-Something-Else-Total-Lack-of-Involvement.

What may escape you in the cloud of excessive blasé you're trying to create is this: You can't win with "I don't care." Watch.

> **"If you don't bring your grades up, we're going to take away your stereo."**

> **"I don't care."**

Let's say your parents believe you. You've just given them permission to do whatever they want.

Now let's say they don't believe you. Instead, they suspect that you say "I don't care" just to thwart them, to make them look for a less painful punishment. Now they're tipped off to the fact that you do care, and they'll stick to their threat like peanut butter to your gums.

Here, too, as you employ more and more of the strategies in this book, you'll outgrow the need to resort to this type of protective move. This is a good thing because a) "I don't care" doesn't work in the first place and b) you'll be bringing up parents who *will* care about the fact that you care. From now on, you'll have much better luck saying:

> **"Wait a minute. I really do care."**

## "You Don't Love Me."

Tsk, tsk. Cheap. Very cheap. You don't really want to play that dirty, do you? Besides, they're just going to respond with:

> *"If we didn't love you, we'd let you do anything.  But we do love you, which is why the answer is no."*

So where does that get you?

## "Well, I Said I'm Sorry."

The reason saying you're sorry works is because it essentially throws you upon the mercy of the court.  Parents like that.  You make yourself vulnerable, like a turtle on its back.

You say:

> *"I'm sorry, I'm sorry."*

The underlying message is:

> *"What else can I do?  I said I'm sorry.  Beat me, torture me, chop me up and serve me as hamburger.  I'm sorry, I'm sorry, what more do you want?"*

Saying you're sorry is a good defensive move, since most reasonable parents will take pity and be most understanding when you aren't posing a threat to them.  For some reason, though, giving light of day to the sentiment, "Well, I *said* I'm sorry," turns an apology into a cop-out, as if it's okay to do anything as long as you apologize for it afterwards.  As if you thought that just because you said you're sorry, that should be the end of it.  (Which is exactly what you did think, but you can't say that.)  The end of it must result from your parents' compassion for you as a reformed sinner begging for their mercy and forgiveness.

## "Nothin'."

> *"What did you do in school today?"*
>
> *"Nothin'."*

*"What on earth is going on in there?"*

*"Nothin'."*

*"Look at you! Your clothes are torn and you're all scratched up. What happened?"*

*"Nothin'."*

Like your parents' "We'll see," the word "Nothin'" means, "The-last-thing-I-want-to-do-right-now-is-answer-your-question." But anythin' is better than nothin'. Throw your parents a few crumbs. They won't feel ignored and hurt. What they will feel is that you're sharing, confiding, and communicating. You can still tell them nothing, which I assume is what you want to say in the first place.

The secret is telling them enough to satisfy the parental "need to know" while cutting things short as if it's only fate (as opposed to a vow on your part) that keeps them uninformed. That way they won't take it personally.

Let's try again with the parental questions from before. Only this time, throw Mom and Dad a few tidbits. For example, in response to "What did you do in school today," you don't have to tell what you and Cindy Lewis did in the janitor's closet during lunch, and you're certainly not going to tell what you and your friends did to Johnny Nerdsky's clothes in the locker room after gym (or, for that matter, what you did to Johnny Nerdsky), and why on earth would you want to mention the chat you had with Mr. Merkle during study hall about "attitude"? No, sirree, the idea is to make your parents feel better, not worse. Offer a smattering of details served up with lilt and enthusiasm.

**Parent Question #1:**

*"What did you do in school today?"*

*"Not much. Got my history test back," (grade revelation optional), "played soccer in gym, Mrs. Bedrock was sick, had a pushover sub, barf-a-roni for lunch, spelling bee in assembly, but, gee, I gotta run now. Talk to you later, Mom."*

Everyone wins. You didn't reveal anything of importance, and your mom is warmed by the details of your life. She can take comfort in the fact that it's your busy lifestyle rather than anything reflecting upon her that cut

communication short. (With any luck, your mom may soon get as bored with your school day as you and stop asking.)

**Parent Question #2:**

*"What on earth is going on in there?"*

*"Oh, sorry, Dad."* Tee hee. Giggles. *"Didn't mean to bother you."* More giggles. *"Guess we just got carried away."* Bug-eyed glances and hand-over-mouth stifled giggles. *"We'll try to be quieter."* Giggles leading to imminent suffocation.

If he only knew. Which he doesn't, because you told him nothing while giving him something: the sense that he exists. Everyone's happy.

**Parent Question #3:**

*"Look at you! Your clothes are torn and you're all scratched up. What happened?"*

*"If you really want to know, remember Eddie Rich? Well, Eddie, he has this cousin who goes to Harley High who met this girl whose roommate visited Laurie Soames last summer, and they got together with Ida May Billings who hates me 'cause she thinks I told Todd Feinstein, who was her boyfriend before Eddie, about what Keith DeWitt said about her after the dance, except it wasn't me, it was Alvin Kramer, who wanted to get back at me for putting bird food in his tuna salad sandwich. Well, anyway, Eddie comes up to me and—"*

*"Look, why don't you just go and clean yourself up. Dinner's almost ready."*

# TROUBLESHOOTING: GETTING TO TROUBLE BEFORE IT GETS TO YOU

## In the Heat of the Fight

The worst time to argue is in the middle of a fight. Problems escalate as hasty and hurtful remarks raise the stakes of damage. Your parents will be most concerned with their authority and your lack of respect. You'll be most concerned with your authority and their lack of respect. With feelings on overload, nobody's going to be open to compromise or to hearing another perspective.

The best thing you can do at these times is to get out of danger. Stop the fight. Don't let it get to the point where battle lines have been drawn, ultimatums issued, or conclusions stated. You can do this in two ways:

1. If you're not past the point of no return, get control of the argument by immediately using conflict-reducing styles of communication: Active Listening and I-messages. This should tone things down and put an end to the name-calling and blame-falling.

2. If you *are* past the point of no return and you and your parents are too upset to come back to the land of the loving, try to remove yourself from the situation. This can be tricky; you need your parents' semi-permission, or you could be up on charges of desertion:

   *"How dare you walk away while we're talking to you?"*

   *"You'll stay right here until I tell you that you can go."*

The best way to make your escape is via a constructive, non-threatening avenue:

   *"Let's not talk anymore until we've had a chance to cool down, okay?"*

*"I'd like to think about this some more. Can we discuss it later?"*

*"Can we talk about this another time, when we're not so angry?"*

The key is in making your suggestion come across as a positive remark and not a dismissal of your parents or the issue. Tabled for discussion until a less testy time.

# "You're Absolutely Right"

This technique is a winner-and-a-half. No, make that two. Next time you're in hot water (deservedly so) and your parents tell you in no uncertain terms what you did wrong, listen quietly and, when they're through, simply tell them:

*"You're absolutely right."*

If they don't fall over in a dead faint, they may reply incredulously:

*"What did you say?"*

This gives you an opportunity for an encore:

*"I said, you're absolutely right."*

Your biggest problem the first few times will be convincing your parents that you mean it.

*"What do you mean, you think we're absolutely right?"*

*"Just that. You're absolutely right."*

*"Right about what?"*

*"Right about _____."* *(Fill in the blank with their assessment of your transgression.)*

These words will sound strange to them for a while. Keep at it. Nothing stops an argument faster than this stance. What can your parents possibly say after you've agreed that they're right? The reason they go on and on is to convince you that they *are* right. If you're convinced, they no longer have any reason to continue.

Because this technique is such a sure-fire, knock-'em-dead squabble-stopper, there is one condition for using it: Your parents have to be absolutely right. Otherwise, you're absolutely wrong to say so.

## Disorienting Parents

One reason "You're Absolutely Right" works so well is that it catches your parents off guard. They're expecting an argument, a denial, a long list of excuses; instead, they get a straightforward admission of culpability. They don't know how to handle it, they're thrown for a loop. So they'll sputter themselves into stunned silence.

The broader strategy here is the value in Disorienting Parents. When you're unpredictable, it's harder for your folks to stereotype you. If you groan and moan every time you're asked to cut the lawn, do it happily one day. If you stomp and sulk when you get a big, fat "no," accept it cheerfully one day. The change in your parents will be remarkable. They'll be thrilled to have avoided the fight they expected to find.

Who knows, if you keep it up, they just may surprise you one day with an unexpected "YES."

## Don't Hook In

This is a further refinement of the Disorienting Parents strategy. The next time they criticize you, don't hook in. Ignore what they say. If they push for some response, use a calm, neutral message:

> *"I'm sorry you feel that way because I can see how much it upsets you."*

Maybe you're thinking, "Well, I'm not going to ignore it. They can't get away with saying things like that about me." If you're a little kid, that's true. You won't let them get away with it. But if you're not a little kid, hooking in only shows that *your parents still control you.* Your anger, defensiveness, and resentment in response to their criticism confirms the power position they occupy.

Do you want to give them that power?  Fine.  Take the bait and get all hyped up to counterattack.

Do you want to show that your opinion of yourself doesn't rise and fall on every word they utter?  That they can't jerk your emotions around like a yo-yo on a string?  Fine.  Then don't grab on, don't hook in.  Let their words pass you by like a lonely cloud in the wind.

## Cut Them Off at the Pass

No teenager likes to be chewed out, but every teenager would admit to having been wrong at least once or having done at least one really dumb thing.

Well, almost every teenager.  Much of the friction in a family exists because parents maintain a vigil in search of their children's wrongdoings. Cutting Them Off at the Pass is a technique that will reward you with a double whammy of benefits:

1.  You'll reduce the number of lectures you receive, and
2.  You'll get your folks to see you as a sensitive, open, self-aware, and mature individual who has sound judgment and is deserving of greater respect and freedom.  (Not bad, eh?)

The idea is this:  If you've done something wrong and you know you're going to get a lecture or scolding (and deserve it), beat your parents to the punch.  It's a lot easier to say, "Boy, was that ever a dumb thing I did," than to hear your parents say, "How could you be so stupid?"

Watch the usual way, then see the difference when this strategy is used.

Your dad has told you a million times not to do bike acrobatics on the lawn.  There's a nearby field where you can ride to your heart's content.  But on this particularly fateful Thursday afternoon, a friend pops by who can only stay for a few minutes.  You want to impress this friend with the latest trick you've mastered.  So you set up a few crates and ramps, pop a wheelie for good measure, and launch your motocross rocket through outer suburban space...only to come to an unceremoniously mortifying splashdown at the feet of your smirking friend.  As if that isn't bad enough, your father's pride-and-joy-freshly-mowed-recently-thatched-perfectly-manicured-lovingly-fertilized-carpet-of-lawn now sports a muddy gash that looks as if it had been the site of the Lilliputian Super Bowl.

**159**

You feel dumb and embarrassed. You're furious with yourself for taking the risk, for showing off, for messing up, for not anticipating what could have happened. Plus your father is going to have an absolute fit when he gets home. He'll see the gash and launch into a tirade. You'll be in no shape to listen calmly. Your guilt will make you feel defensive, and you'll be likely to strike back and get into even more trouble. See how easy it is for that to happen...

*"TOBY!!!! Get down here this instant!"*

*"Oh, hi, Dad. Didn't hear you come home. What is it?"*

*"You know perfectly well what it is! Just look at the lawn! How did that happen?"*

*"Well...er...it was...well...you see, I was trying to do this trick and—"*

*"How many times have I told you there is to be no bike riding on the lawn? HOW MANY??"*

*"Lots."*

*"And you just ignore me? There is a field two blocks away. Are you so overworked that you can't go two blocks to ride your bike? Most kids would dream of having a bike like yours and all I ask is one thing, that you don't ride on the lawn. Is that too much to ask?"*

*"No, but I didn't mean to, I mean, I was just going to do one trick so I didn't think—"*

*"Exactly. You didn't think. Don't you ever think? Sometimes I wonder if you think of anyone else in the world except yourself. I'm taking your bike away and you're going to have to—"*

*"That's not fair! It's just a stupid lawn anyway. You care more about your dumb lawn than you do about me. Why do you have to have perfect grass? No one else does."*

*"That's enough out of you. You go to the garage this instant and bring me your bike. When you show me that you can think of someone besides yourself, you'll get it back."*

*"Dad, I'll fix the lawn, but I'm not giving you my bike."*

*"You'll do as you're told. Get it, NOW!!"*

*"Dad—"*

*"NOW!!!!!!"*

Oh dear.

Your dad has every right to be angry. But his attack hurts (he hasn't learned to communicate his feelings without attacking you), you're defensive, and before you know it, everything is out of control.

What happens when you use the Cut Them Off at the Pass technique? First, you get to him *before* he sees the lawn. Maybe you watch for him to come home, or call him at work if you know he won't mind. The idea is that you're going to say the things you know he would say. You're going to anticipate his reaction and feelings and do his work for him. That should leave him with little else to add.

*"Dad, I did a really dumb thing today. I don't know what came over me. I guess I was showing off for a friend who couldn't stay long and I wanted to do just one trick on my bike so I didn't go to the field like I'm supposed to and instead I did it at home and I'm afraid I put a little...well, I guess it was kind of a big gash in the lawn. I know how mad you must be" (don't give him a chance to get a word in) "and I know you've told me a million times not to ride on the lawn and I shouldn't have done it. I'm really sorry but I'll fix it. I've watched you and I know how to reseed it. I'll do it tomorrow. I guess you're pretty mad."*

*"Toby, you know you're not supposed to ride on the lawn. But at least you know that what you did was wrong, and I'm glad you told me what happened. I suppose if you take care of it there's not much else I can say."*

*"I'll do it first thing after school tomorrow."*

*"All right. And Toby?"*

*"Yeah?"*

*"Don't ride on the lawn. You know how much it means to me."*

*"I know. Sorry."*

**161**

There, wasn't that better? Just look at the power you have when you show your parents that you understand their feelings. They rant and rave in order to get their point across; if you state it for them, they won't have to. That's the whole idea behind this valuable strategy. You avoid the lecture, you 'fess up to a mess up, and as part of the bargain, you impress upon your parents the maturity and honesty of their child. Not bad for a few minutes' time.

## Agree to Disagree

### *"My parents and I disagree about everything."*

Why shouldn't you? You were raised by different people, grew up in different environments, and were exposed to different cultural and societal values. It would be surprising if you didn't have disagreements about clothes, friends, music, and the worthiness of various pursuits.

While it stands to reason that you'd have different tastes, opinions, and attitudes, problems arise because many parents judge the success of their parenting (and their children) by the degree to which their kids share their own interests and values. Parental authority becomes threatened when you embrace other opinions and reject theirs.

Your parents' identities consist in large part of their likes and dislikes, their attitudes and values. When you reject something they value, they feel that you've rejected them. This is why they're so insistent that there's the *right* way to do something (that's how *they* do it) and the *wrong* way (that's how *you* do it). Their desire to have you share their tastes is matched only by your desire not to. This sets the stage for critical judgments and personality slurs.

**"How can you listen to such trash?"**

**"Why do you spend so much time with that jerk?"**

**"How can you waste your money on such junk?"**

But one person's junk is another person's treasure, and nothing will change the fact that you and your parents are going to disagree often. What you need to do, then, is encourage a new attitude in your parents towards disagreement. Instead of the way it is now—where disagreement means that someone's right, someone's wrong, something's better, and something's worse—you need to generate a climate in which differences can be seen as positive, and where there can be respect for another position.

The way to pull it off? Agree to Disagree. Here's how.

Next time there's a clash of styles that threatens to launch World War III, don't try to convince your parents (or yourself) that one vision is better than another. You may feel that way, but that's not the point. You may not respect your parents' choice, but you can respect their individuality and their right to choose. That's the attitude you'll need to extend in order to break this negative cycle of judgment and put-downs.

Watch how most households handle disagreement:

**"How can you listen to such trash?"**

**"It's not trash. This is the Number One album in the country."**

**"That just goes to show that the country's going down the drain."**

*"At least it's a lot better than the stuff you and Mom listen to."*

*"Don't talk back to me, young lady."*

*"Well, don't you say my music is trash."*

*"Don't tell me what I can and can't say. This is my house and if I don't want that noise blasting away under my roof, you're not going to play it."*

*"You can't tell me what music to play. This is my room and you can't even hear it in the hall."*

*"I don't like your attitude one bit...."*

And on and on.

Now watch the difference when a clever kid refuses to take the bait and instead whips out the Agree to Disagree strategy.

*"How can you listen to such trash?" (This is the moment of truth. Will the kid stoop to her father's level or elevate the interaction to her level?)*

*"I guess you don't like this music, eh, Dad?" (Bravo! She didn't hook in. She used Active Listening and is reflecting her dad's feelings back to him.)*

*"Don't like it? I wouldn't even call it music." (Dad continues to try to establish the supremacy of his position. His daughter is too smart to fall for it.)*

*"You've got to admit that the music you and Mom listen to isn't exactly my favorite, either. But that's okay. We have different tastes, that's all. You listen to the music you like, and I'll listen to the music I like. Okay?" (Now, how can Dad object to such a reasonable position?)*

*"I guess so. Just keep it down."*

Whew! That was much easier. What happened this time around?

1. The daughter didn't lash back at her father, as in the first exchange.
2. The daughter showed that she understood her father's attitude. (She didn't agree, but she felt no need to convert him to her opinion. After all, that's what he tries to do to her.)
3. The daughter kept things calm and proposed the notion that it's all right for two people to have different tastes without one's having to be better than the other's.
4. The argument was defused because the father felt heard. Three cheers for the daughter!

Note that agreeing to disagree works best when the conflict is over different tastes, styles, opinions, or ideas—situations where no thwarting of another's needs occurs, and no action or follow-through is required. Obviously, if you want to go to a party and your parents say "no," agreeing to disagree doesn't address the conflict. Or if they forbid you to watch TV until your grades improve, you can't just say, "Okay, let's agree to disagree; you think I shouldn't watch TV and I think I should, so I will and we'll agree to disagree." Problems like these require direct solving, since both positions can't exist at the same time. But any problem in which one person's opinion needn't affect the other (for example, they like Beethoven and you don't) is prime grist for this mill.

So when it comes to matters of taste, opinion, politics, and personal style, move your parents to a position where they can respect your right to have preferences by extending to them their right to do the same.

Some lines you can put into your own words and use to accomplish this would include:

*"Why don't we just agree to disagree?"*

*"Let's not fight. You have your opinion and I have mine. That's all."*

*"I respect your right to have your own likes and dislikes. I'd like to feel that you can respect mine."*

*"Just because we have different tastes doesn't mean one of us has to be wrong. We're just different."*

*"Ah, diversity of opinion is what makes America great, don't you think, Mom?"*

# Admit You're Out to Lunch

You told your mother you wished she were dead. You blabbed to your friends the contents of your sister's diary. You kicked a hole in the TV screen in a fit of anger. You're giving your parents the silent treatment because they won't let you go on a school trip to New York City.

Sometimes you will go bonkers. You'll be off the wall, off your rocker, blinded by emotion, carried away by the seductive hands of a hidden agenda. Mathematical probability says so (even if you don't).

While everyone is allowed a moment of temporary insanity, your bread will be better buttered if you can minimize the occasions when this occurs. Those states of being crucial to your freedom—such as trustworthiness, good judgment, open-mindedness, responsibility (blah, blah, blah)—depend on keeping down the number of times when you do indeed lunch out. You don't want to come across as an airhead. If you suspect that there may be a few screws loose in the cabinet of your corpus callosum, tighten them up. Here's how:

1. Let some time pass. You may feel different in the morning if your position was caused by transitory stress or emotional blind-siding.

2. Ask the opinion of a neutral observer.

3. Often, there won't be a neutral observer. There might be a biased observer or no one at all who was party to the incident. In that case, find someone whose opinion you respect and lay out the facts. Be truthful—try not to use words or details to sway the verdict. If you bias a listener, the opinion you get won't be of much value.

4. Check far and wide for any hidden agendas that may be influencing you.

5. Reverse the situation. Privately, so no one need know how open you are to the possibility that you could be wrong, switch positions with your parents in your head. Try to imagine how you would feel if they did to you what you did to them, how you would react if they said to you what you said to them. It may be hard to reverse some situations because they're so specific to parent and child roles. If so, try to imagine an analogous scenario involving your friends.

Don't be afraid to discover that you were out to lunch. That only means that you now have a wonderful opportunity to stage a comeback by dazzling your folks with a note, an Act of Goodness, an apology, a logical consequence of your own choosing. You'll be welcomed back to the land of rational behavior with open and admiring arms.

# The Trial Period

*"Living with my parents is one big trial, period!"*

I know how it is. So here's another strategy for bringing up parents who will get off your case, judge you innocent until proven guilty, and stop laying down the law 24 hours a day. If your folks court disaster by overly protective custody, you'll need to spring to your own defense. Suggest a Trial Period.

Parents often object to what you want to do and what you want to have because of what they *fear* might happen.

*"You'll be too tired for school."* **(No I won't.)**

*"You're not strong enough yet."* **(Yes I am.)**

*"You'll get bored with it."* **(I will not.)**

*"Your brother will object."* **(How do you know?)**

*"It'll take too much time."* **(Who says?)**

When you're face-to-face with those arguments that hinge on whether something will or won't happen, enter into a trial period so you can find out what does, in fact, happen. This strategy can be used for many common household conflicts including curfews, bedtimes, going out, friends coming over, TV watching, and homework.

Let's say you want to get an after-school job. Your parents won't let you because they're afraid it will take too much time away from schoolwork. They're sure your grades will go down and you'll be tired the next day from staying up later. You say that you do have the time, your grades will be fine, and you won't get tired.

Instead of arguing over who's right and who's wrong, agree to a trial period. For six weeks, or one grading period, you'll be allowed to have an after-school job. If your grades go down or you start to fall asleep in school

(which isn't hard to do under the best circumstances), you'll give up the job. If everything goes well, you'll be permitted to keep it.

For trial periods to work, you and your parents must agree to two conditions:

1. Your parents must make every effort to support your success, or at least remain neutral. No sabotage allowed—no extra chores or new conditions, no changing rules midstream.

2. You must cheerfully go back to how things were if the trial period doesn't confirm your predictions.

Trial periods work to your advantage. Most parents are afraid to extend new freedoms because, once extended, they're almost impossible to take back. A trial period, if you play by the rules, sets their minds at ease. That's because you're saying, "If I'm not ready for this freedom, I'll give it back." That's why the conditions above are so important. In exchange for your parents' willingness to go out on a limb by allowing you a freedom they're not sure you should have, you're agreeing to give it back if things don't work out. That seems only fair.

CAUTION: Don't enter into trial periods recklessly, thinking, "Oh, it doesn't matter, once I start doing this they'll let me continue no matter what." The whole point with a trial is to prove *you* correct. Don't try it if there's a good chance you're wrong. Your parents will be more willing to allow future test situations and extend greater freedom if each trial period goes smoothly and their fears don't come true. Trial periods are a great way to show your responsibility, your keen judgment, and the accuracy of your self-awareness. If that's what your parents see, they'll be happy to be proven wrong.

## The Respectable Lie

We've got to be careful here. I'm about to say that there are times when it's okay to lie. And I want to be absolutely, positively sure that you don't take it as a license to lie. If you're still with me—if you agree to those terms—read on. Otherwise, skip to the next section because the strategy I'm about to describe just won't work for you.

Sometimes, telling the truth, the whole truth, and nothing but the truth to your parents does more harm than good. While honesty is the best policy 99 out of 100 times, so is not hurting someone else. Occasionally, the two can conflict.

Generally speaking, teenagers lie for two reasons:

1. To keep from getting in trouble, and/or

2. To be able to do things they want to do that their parents won't let them do.

These would be *un*respectable lies:

*"Clarence, did you take five dollars out of my purse?"*

*"No, I didn't, Mom." LIE!!!*

*"Felicia, where are you going?"*

*"I'm spending the night at Sally's." LIE!!!*

These unrespectable lies erode your parents' trust and your self-esteem. When you're caught, you not only have the original trouble you would have been in, but the added trouble from your lie.

For a lie to have a chance at respectability, two conditions must be met:

1. The lie is told to avoid hurting someone's feelings, and
2. Telling the truth would serve no constructive purpose.

Not all lies meeting these criteria are respectable, though. The main idea here is this: Don't be honest to a fault. There's a lot in your parents' styles, tastes, opinions, and habits that you won't like. But that doesn't mean you have to go out of your way (like some kids do) to make sure (for the sake of honesty) that your parents know how you feel, even if they ask you.

Consider your mother's new haircut—the one she likes so much. Does it really matter whether she knows how horrible you think it is? What purpose would be served in telling her? If put on the spot, you can boldly lie or tactfully dance around the truth:

**"How do you like my new haircut?"**

**"Looks great, Mom." LIE!!!**

But respectable because of the boost to Mom's self-image and the lack of purpose served by saying, "I hate it." (Leave that to your father.)

Or:

**"Wow, it's really something else!"**

Or, if you have to tell the truth, at least say:

**"It's not my style, but I'm glad you like it so much."**

Now, I can just picture some of you out there saying, "It's about time someone spoke up for lying! After all, I lie all the time. I'd never want to hurt my parents by letting them know all the things I do. I'm much too considerate for that."

That's precisely the attitude I'm afraid of. Of course it hurts your parents to learn that you stole, or skipped school, or took the car without permission (or a license, if you want to be technical). But it will hurt them a lot more to find out that you lied and that your relationship is based on dishonesty. If you're constantly lying to stay out of trouble, you're already in trouble.

There's one more instance where lies can be respectable. This instance is even more vulnerable to misuse by teenage truth-abusers. But I'll risk the possibility that a few of you will hear what I'm saying as blanket permission to lie in the hope that most of you will be honest with yourselves and your motivations for lying.

It's okay to lie IF your parents have taken a position affecting your life that is:

- cruel,
- objectively unrealistic,
- patently unreasonable,
- harmful to your future,
- harmful to your emotional well-being,
- categorically neurotic or pathological, and/or
- clearly deviant from the norms of their peers,
  AND:
- you have tried your best to alter their position without any success,
  AND:
- there is no way that you can or would alter your position without causing great personal harm to yourself,
  AND:
- your being truthful about your disobedience would result in extreme, unfair, or even brutal punishment.

If *all* of these conditions are *fully* met, then your lie can be a respectable one.

> **"No problem. This definition fits all of my parents' positions. Like when they wouldn't let me have a motorcycle for my ninth birthday, or let me and my girl go to the beach for the weekend, or—"**

NO, NO, NO!

I really have to appeal to your integrity and sense of fair play with this definition. I know there are times when your parents' refusals to let you go to a party or keep your room however you want seem like cruel and unusual punishment. But it only seems that way. It really isn't that way. (And you know it, too.) I'm talking about times when it doesn't just seem that way, but really is that way. I'm talking about situations where a kid has a parent who really is Out Of Touch With Reality.

This example should give you an idea of the type of situation I have in mind. Let's say you're a 16-year-old girl and your father will not let you be alone with boys, talk on the telephone to boys, or write letters to boys. He forbids you to have any interaction with them at all, except for school (which is a girls' school anyway) or when he is physically present. He watches you like a hawk, he's been known to follow you to check up, and he only lets you go over to girlfriends' houses because your mom (at great risk to herself) makes him. You've tried talking to him, to your mom, but nothing works. He's closed to any discussion, and he has made it quite clear that if he ever catches you with a boy, he'll whup your hide.

This behavior is not normal. Your healthy and timely social and emotional growth will be thwarted by his problem. In a case like this, I think you have a right to lie. If you go for a walk after school with some girlfriends and a couple of boys and your father asks what you did after school, this is what you might say:

*"I went for a walk with my friends."*

*"You're sure you weren't out with boys?"*

*"I'm sure." LIE!!! But a respectable one, under the circumstances.*

Of course, you run the risk of getting caught. But you're already at risk from having to live with someone so mixed-up. At rare times, you do have to lie to protect yourself, your rights, your future.

But please be careful with the respectable lie. I've respected you enough to include it here.

## Give Up on Lost Causes

I know all about the stigma of being a quitter, of walking away from the battlefield. It's just not the American Way. But if you're really smart, you'll make it your way. Learn the fine art of quitting. It can be an act of strength and cunning.

There are two prime times for giving up:

1. When you're wrong, and
2. When you're right.

172

While the times that you're wrong may occur with the frequency of Halley's Comet, when they do occur, give up, let go. Ranting, raving, pushing, and defending when you're out to lunch, unreasonable, pig-headed, selfish, inconsiderate, or obnoxious does not do much for your image. It does not do much towards convincing your parents how wise, reasonable, responsible, and self-aware you really are—a conviction they must possess if you are to bring them up properly. So when you're wrong, don't stick to a foolish position out of pride. Just forget it. Back off. Shut up. Go away.

Come back. Apologize, admit your mistake, write a loving note, send flowers. You'll be in Fat City! If there's one thing parents love more than a perfect child, it's an imperfect one who can admit to an error.

The second occasion that calls for giving up is when you're right. Assume that your parents are displaying more than their usual amount of silliness and irrationality. Assume that the situation is one in which most people would say that your position is reasonable, and your parents are wrong in their unwillingness to compromise or look at it from your perspective. Further assume that the situation, while insulting your intelligence and sense of fairness, just isn't That Big a Deal.

Give up—even though you're right. Save your strength for the really important issues where you must never give up. Let your parents hold a wrong opinion, let them mix up their facts and times and dates. Let them be unreasonable. You'll need to preserve your strength for those times when giving up would be tantamount to surrendering the adolescent species to unbridled parental power.

An example of a good time to give up would be: Your father won't let you walk around the house barefoot. Your mother couldn't care less (in fact, she's somewhat pleased that you're not stomping through the house with muddy shoes), but for some reason, the old man has a hissy whenever he sees your naked feet.

You've explained everything to him: the comforts of bare feet, the money he saves because your shoes won't wear out as quickly, the labor (and odor) spared by fewer socks in the laundry room, your right to freedom of toe expression, and, most critically, the spiritual lift you receive from this communion with Rousseaunian values of Natural Man. All to no avail. He just mutters on about "...no child of mine..." and "...scruffy little beggars..." and "...that's that..." and "...no more discussion."

Of course he's being ridiculous, but that doesn't mean you have to join in. Why hook into a minor issue and have a major fight? Don't jump into a lost cause. Toe the line and wait for a worthier battle. Toss a pair of shoes on your feet when the Great Irrational One is around the house, take 'em off when he's gone, and congratulate yourself on being smart enough to...

## Allow Dad His Neurosis

It's a lot easier to let go of an issue if you don't see it as your *defeat* and your parents' *victory*. Instead, simply decide that your parents, possibly a bit more than most people, have neuroses—lapses of sound judgment and objective thought, unexplainable behaviors that appear irrational and obsessive—in short, your folks are going to sing a looney tune now and then.

It is precisely because their attitude or action is neurotic that you should give up. Exercise your superior insight on these trivial matters. Reason and rational discussion are not possible when a neurosis is afoot in your parents' kingdom. Who knows why your dad is uptight about bare feet? Maybe he grew up so poor he couldn't afford shoes, or his feet were saved from being steamrolled into tomorrow's soup by a pair of steel-toed boots. Whatever the case, he probably doesn't know either, and will try to mask his neurosis with logic and parental rights.

Give it up. It's not worth it. You'd encourage him to give up if the neurosis were on the other foot.

A note on execution: It's perfectly fine to say:

> *"Dad, I don't agree with you about wearing shoes in the house at all. But since it's so important to you, I've decided to go along."*

You'll be able to cash in the points gained here for something more important some other time.

If you hesitate to give up on lost causes, even when you're right, it's because of one thing, *pride*. Well, don't worry. You don't have to let your pride get in the way. Your father is sure to bring more than enough for both of you.

# Chapter 5

# CLOSE ENCOUNTERS OF THE WORST KIND:

## SOLVING FAMILY PROBLEMS

# A FEW AT A TIME

You look around and see nothing but problems. Conflict behind you, conflict to the right, conflict to the left, and conflict dead ahead. It's hopeless, overwhelming, everything's a mess, you don't even know where to begin. If you're like most people, you'll get so frustrated by the magnitude of the task that you'll never begin. It's too much.

It *is* too much. You can't solve 100 problems at once. But you can solve *one* problem. And when that one's solved, you can solve one more. And bit by bit, one at a time, you'll cross all sorts of troubling issues off your list, issues that would still be there if you tried to take them all on at once.

So, choose one problem that's bothering you. Not the hardest one, not the deepest one, not the trickiest or most emotionally charged one. Just a good old solid, reasonable problem. You might want to sit down with your parents and decide which problem to tackle.

Once you've identified the guinea-pig problem, do some intelligence-gathering. Understand the nature of the issue: the people, the needs, the feelings involved, the points of conflict, the points of agreement. Then decide how you want to deal with it. A talk? A note? An apology? A trial period? A Problem-Solving Session? Do you want to discuss it with a friend, a sibling? Do you want to change your behavior and see what happens? Choose your approach or combination of approaches. Then go for it.

Once you've solved that problem, choose another. If you solved just one problem a month, you'd have 12 fewer by the end of the year. Why, if you solved just one problem every two weeks, you could handle over 26 in a year's time. A problem a week? Holy dilemma! That's 52 in a year. In fact, if you really got rolling and solved a problem a day, you'd take care of 365—well, we'll give you your birthday off—364 problems a year. That's so many problems, you might have to invent some just to keep your docket full.

# STRIKE BARGAINS, OFFER ALTERNATIVES

Most arguments go like this:

*Arguer 1: This is My Position.*

*Arguer 2: This is MY Position!*

*Arguer 1: I said, you imbecile, that this is MY POSITION!!*

*Arguer 2: And I said, you moron, that this is MY POSITION!!!*

*Arguer 1: You're wrong!!!!*

*Arguer 2: You're wronger!!!!!*

*Arguer 1: You're the wrongest!!!!!!*

*Arguer 2: You're too stupid to even know!!!!!!!*

*Arguer 1: Who are you calling stupid, you jerk????!!!!*

*Arguer 2: You, but you're obviously too stupid to realize it!!!!!!!!*

*Arguer 1: Well, I'm right and I'm not giving one inch!!!!!!!!*

*Arguer 2: I'M right and I'M not giving one half-inch!!!!!!!!*

The I-Win, You-Lose mentality of problem-solving is so prevalent in our culture that many opportunities for settling disputes are overlooked. It's as if people would prefer *all* of *nothing* to *some* of *everything*.

*"If I can't have it my way, forget it."*

This self-defeating position fails to recognize three important concepts:

1. Reality,
2. Human nature, and
3. The fine art of negotiation.

- *Reality* teaches that issues are rarely black-or-white, all-or-nothing. There are often several valid ways to look at the same situation.

- *Human nature* teaches that people (parents) don't like to feel as if they've been had. Yet people (parents) are often quite willing to give ground if they feel that other people (their children) are willing to do the same.

- *Negotiation* teaches that the best way to get what you want is to make it appear that you're letting the other person get his or her way while actually giving up nothing.

This is the secret to the fine art of negotiating with your parents:

- Discover something they want that you don't care that much about, then

- Agree to let them have it.

They'll be impressed by your willingness to compromise. (They don't have to know that it wasn't that big a deal to you.) Now, because of your graciousness, they'll be more inclined to make a concession and let you have something important.

Instead of getting bogged down in a dead-end disagreement, search for those areas of the dispute where:

1. You can agree,
2. You aren't that invested, and
3. You're willing to compromise.

This is where intelligence-gathering and hidden-agenda-hunting come in. You must understand your parents' motives and feelings to be an artful negotiator. Your parents' objections, once known, may be easily addressed by striking a bargain. If you agree to come home an hour earlier, they'll agree to let you go. If you agree to spend an hour a day reading a book, they'll agree to forget about summer school. Don't lose it all because you're not willing to lose a little. Don't get backed into a cul-de-sac of conflict; steer for those crossroads of compromise. You'll end up traveling much farther down the freedom trail.

# MOTHER, PLEASE!
# I'D RATHER DO IT MYSELF!

You broke the lamp. You forgot to turn off the water in the bathtub and flooded the house. You accidentally deleted all of your dad's computer files.

So, there you are. Feeling rotten. Surrounded by Trouble with a Capital T. You're full of guilt, you want to make amends, to find a way out of your tunnel of regret. You're all set to right the wrong, to take an action, to suggest a solution, and what happens? Your parents barge in with an armful of how-to's and oughta-shoulds, telling you exactly what to do.

Their ideas are going to be either:

1. Off the wall, in which case they should be ignored, or
2. The same as yours, in which case they *must* be ignored.

By trying to do your thinking and solving for you, parents cheat you of many things:

- the confidence that comes from knowing you can handle your own problems,
- the opportunity to say, "I did it myself," and
- the chance to feel better and lessen guilt by showing that you cared enough to find a solution without being told.

These same parents who want to take over for you now will also turn around much later to say:

> **"Why don't you ever think for yourself?"**

> **"Why can't you be more self-sufficient and independent?"**

Bringing up parents who let you do it yourself should be high on your priority list. If your problem is a personal one and you don't want your parents' help, tell them. Use an I-message so they won't have a cow. It could go something like this:

> **"I know you're anxious to help, and I appreciate that, but I'd rather know I can take care of it myself. Thanks anyway."**

If your parents are mixed up in the problem but you'd still prefer to solve it yourself, give 'em another I-message. If you're the one at fault, you could say:

*"I got us into this mess. I'd like to get us out of it."*

Or:

*"I'd feel better if I solved this problem, since it was my fault in the first place."*

If you share the problem and they're trying to impose a solution you can't support, you might say:

*"I'd really like to have a chance to come up with some ideas for solving this problem myself."*

Your folks may come back at you with:

*"We were only trying to help."*

Or:

*"Well, if you don't care to benefit from our wisdom...."*

If this happens, use Active Listening skills. Find their feelings and reflect them back:

*"Sounds like I've hurt your feelings."*

*"I bet you feel I don't care what you think."*

Then, as they respond, shift back and forth between Active Listening and nice, easy-going, nonthreatening I-messages until you see your folks out of their crisis.

# FOCUS ON THE FUTURE, NOT ON THE PAST

What's done is done. Let bygones be bygones. It's all water over the dam by now. With so many clichés saying the same thing, there's got to be some truth to this notion.

The past should perform two functions:

1.  Provide a lush cushion of memories to loll in, and
2.  Serve, via experience and error, as a guide for the future.

Parents, however, seem to have latched on to a third function for the past:

3.  Ammunition.

It's as if they have a database of everything you've ever done, all cross-referenced and randomly accessed, ready to call up in a micro-second to use against you.

While there are lessons to be learned from the past, there can't possibly be as many as your parents think. Just when you're ready to let go of an outmoded behavior, they remind you of it. It's enough to make you hang on to it a little longer.

Encourage your parents to look to the future and leave the past behind. It's hard to solve problems when you're focused on what went wrong, on how it didn't work. That only leads to blaming and shaming. You'll all be better equipped for problem-solving if you fix your gaze on the days to come.

*"What can we do from now on?"*

*"How can we prevent that from happening again?"*

*"That's all behind us. What steps can we take now?"*

The past should serve as a handy hook for insight, not a coat rack for fault-finding.

# CRIME AND PUNISHMENT

Admittedly, if Dostoevsky had titled his book, *Crime and Logical Consequences,* it might not have done so well in the marketplace. Families, however, would be well-advised to explore the use of logical consequences in place of punishments as they write the books of their own trials and tribulations.

What's the difference?

## Punishments

Punishments are meant to punish. To get back at. To hurt. They rarely have anything to do with the nature of your "crime." Punishments humiliate, frighten, and demean. Punishments emphasize the power of the parent and the defenselessness of the child. Punishments are based on threats and revenge.

*"We'll show you."*

*"You're a bad person."*

*"This is just what you deserve."*

Punishments make you feel afraid, hurt, guilty, unloved. Punishments lead to rebellion, dishonesty, a desire to get even.

Ultimately, punishments don't work, for sooner or later the day comes when you refuse to submit to them. You hit back, you storm out of the house instead of going to your room, you meet with your friends after school even though you're grounded. As your parents escalate their punishments, you increase your defiance. The relationship has come to a dead end of fear and mistrust.

Punishments place the responsibility for your actions on others. Instead of developing self-discipline and your own sense of conscience and morality, you learn to think of your behavior in terms of what you can get away with. If the way your parents punish you is leading to hostility and rebellion, to bigger threats and deeper mistrust, it's time for you to take the lead and introduce the notion of logical consequences to your family.

# Logical Consequences*

Logical consequences are based in reality. Logical consequences say, "Hey, you did something that wasn't too cool; this is how the cookie's going to crumble as a result." Logical consequences treat you with respect; they separate you and your action—you're a good person who did a bad thing. Logical consequences are related to the misbehavior. They undo damage, restore dignity, and teach you to make choices and be responsible for yourself. Logical consequences are based on trust and good faith; they leave no bitter aftertaste.

Look at the following "crimes" and you'll see the difference between a punishment and a logical consequence.

*The phrase "Natural and Logical Consequences" is attributed to Rudolf Dreikurs.

| The Crime | A Punishment | A Logical Consequence |
|---|---|---|
| Breaking a window in a fit of anger. | Not being allowed to go to a party. | Fixing the window and paying for the materials yourself. |
| Coming home late for dinner. | Having to come straight home from school. | Eating cold food. Going hungry. |
| Hitting your brother. | Dad beats you up. | Doing something nice for your brother: taking him to a movie, playing a game with him. |
| Lying to your parents. | Getting spanked. | Losing your parents' trust. Losing privileges and freedoms that require their trust. |
| Not doing chores. | Being grounded. | Having to pay for the person your parents hire to do your jobs. |

The use of logical consequences doesn't mean you get off easy. You'll feel the impact of a logical consequence in your wallet, in your parents' loss of trust, in diminished freedom, in reduced options. But logical consequences treat you with respect and present you with choices, not threats. If you choose repeatedly to come home after your curfew, you will lose the freedom of staying out late. Once you choose to come home on time, your responsibility will return the freedom to you. You hold all the cards. It's your choice.

Sometimes, it's tricky to come up with a logical consequence. You may have difficulty finding a direct result of your action. Let's say you're being rude, sullen, and abusive towards your parents. (I think they call it "bad attitude.") Your parents are hopping mad. What could a logical consequence of your behavior be? Well, in the "real world," you'd find that people don't like to be around jerks. You might find that your family decides to go to the beach

without you, or to see a movie and leave you behind. But it's made clear to you that as soon as you resume being your usually cheerful and pleasant self, they'll be delighted to enjoy your company once more.

Logical consequences challenge your creativity. They give you much more responsibility and decision-making power. They prepare you for adult life. If you're late for work all the time when you're on your own, your boss isn't going to send you to detention or take away driving privileges. Your boss is going to fire you. If you have a "bad attitude" towards your spouse, you're not going to get your allowance docked for a month. You're going to get served with divorce papers.

Everyone in your family will gain from the use of logical consequences instead of punishments. Your parents will be delighted to see you take more responsibility for your actions and for assuming the burden of their consequences. You will find ways to be more self-disciplined and to make choices to increase your freedom and privileges.

# YOU SHOW ME YOURS AND I'LL SHOW YOU MINE: THE HIDDEN AGENDA

The Hidden Agenda. No, it's not a new-wave band nor a hazard to avoid when you're driving. It's one of the greatest obstacles to problem-solving and clear communication you and your parents will ever meet. It's also a great challenge to your intelligence-gathering skills.

The hidden agenda is everything you don't see, it's everything that isn't said. You may not even know it's there. But it can make it impossible to solve a problem or understand someone's feelings.

So often when people fight, they're not sure what it is they're fighting about. They may not even be fighting about the same thing. It's as if the conflict becomes a symbol, a stand-in for another and sometimes deeper issue. If you can discover the hidden agenda undermining or creating a conflict, you'll be well on the road to faster and easier problem-solving.

Hidden agendas can exist for many reasons:

- People don't always understand their true feelings and impulses.
- People may be embarrassed or ashamed to reveal how they feel.
- People listen through their own "filters" and may not hear what someone else is *really* saying.

Hidden agendas can also come from positive, caring motivations. A desire to help, to love, to give, to support, to avoid hurt. These can be just as dangerous, though, if they go unrecognized.

By now, you can see that hidden agendas come in far more than 57 varieties. They can be emotional (as in a secret fear) or practical (as in an undisclosed need). They can be unconscious or conscious. They can exist in what you say, what you want, what you fight about. If you are to improve family communication, reduce the number of arguments, and bring up parents who respect your feelings and rights, you must be on the lookout for hidden agendas.

Let's expose some common hidden agendas lurking behind your parents' actions and attitudes. They include:

- A need to assert power and control.
- A need to feel needed.
- Anxieties over aging.
- A desire to impress friends or relatives. ("What will the neighbors think?")
- Money.
- Fear.
- Mistrust.
- A reaction to or compensation for something in their childhood.
- Jealousy.
- A feeling of inadequacy.
- A need to appease the other parent.

Do any of these sound familiar? You may already suspect that some of these feelings and motivations are at play in your household.

Let's say your parents won't let you date, even though all of your friends have been dating for two years by now. Whenever you argue about it, your parents just say that you're too young and that's that. Is there a hidden agenda? Probably. What is it? Can't say for sure. It could be that your parents have a need to keep you in the nest as long as possible. Dating symbolizes your growing up (and their growing older). If they restrict you and keep a "baby" in their family, they can't be so old themselves.

Maybe your parents worry that you'll get pregnant or get someone pregnant. Or that you'll get AIDS. If these subjects have never been talked about, either one could be a hidden agenda. If you don't date, they figure, it can't happen. (Yet another example of how silly parents can be. Someone better wise them up.)

You can see how hard it would be to solve this conflict if you and your folks came to it with different hidden agendas. The problem will be solved only when everyone can deal with the real issues and feelings.

Suppose your parents insist that you go to bed at 10:00 on school nights. You think that's ridiculous for someone your age. Your parents say that you need your sleep and that your schoolwork will suffer. That's the level on which the argument takes place. You say:

**_"I'm never tired and my schoolwork is fine."_**

That doesn't satisfy them, and pretty soon a classic power struggle is underway:

**_"We decide your bedtime."_**

**_"You have no right."_**

**_"You'll do what we say."_**

**_"You can't force me to sleep."_**

And so on. Could there be hidden agendas at work here? Naturally. Could it be that your parents like to go to bed early and can't sleep until the house is closed down? (Parent nature, you know.) Or maybe they're afraid that your younger siblings won't go to bed if you're allowed to stay up later. Or perhaps your parents want some private time together for some mysterious reason and would like to get you out of their hair. (Well, no one said a hidden agenda has to be plausible!) Only by uncovering the hidden agenda can you solve the problem.

In this case, you might work things out by agreeing to assume responsibility for putting your siblings to bed in exchange for no bedtime hour. Or you might agree to stay in your room after 10:00 to give your parents the sense of calm or privacy they desire. You can see how arguing a case based on the rights of a teenager or how late your friends stay up is not going to address your parents' hidden agenda.

Before you think you're off the hook, here are some hidden agendas that might be at work in your actions and attitudes:

- A desire to shock, to get a rise out of your folks.
- A desire to test, to see how far you can go.
- A need to feel trusted or loved.
- A need for attention or intervention.
- A desire to impress other kids.
- A desire to assert independence.
- Fear, insecurity, jealousy.
- A desire for revenge.

You ask your father if you can have a beer; you can't stand the stuff, but your hidden agenda is to see how he'll react.

You get in a fight with a friend because you want to sit next to his girlfriend in math. It's not that you like her (which is what he thinks). It's that she's the smartest girl in the class and you want to copy her answers. (No one ever said hidden agendas were moral or lofty.)

You just joined the stamp club because the boy you love madly is in it. He doesn't know that you couldn't give a lick about stamps, and there's no need for him to know. You're under no obligation to tell anyone your inner feelings or motivations. But *you* need to recognize the secret reason behind your action to keep a check on your expectations and strategies. Otherwise, who knows what sort of a sticky situation you could get into.

Look, Jane, look. See another hidden agenda in action:

*"Mom, can I go to the movies Friday night?"*

*"I don't think so, Megan. You've been sick all week, and I think you should get as much rest as possible."*

*"But I feel fine. I went to school today and my fever's gone."*

*"I don't think it's a good idea. You can go next Friday."*

*"But I want to go this Friday. I ought to know how I feel, and I feel fine."*

*"I'm sorry, but the answer's no. You're just getting over strep throat, and you should take it easy. I'm sure your friends will understand."*

*"Well, I'm sorry, too, but I'm going.  You have no right to make me stay home on a Friday night."*

*"I'm not going to argue.  You heard me."*

Seems straightforward enough, doesn't it?  Unh-unh.  There's a raging hidden agenda right below the surface of this brewing brouhaha.  Unknown to you and the mother is the fact that *Megan already told her friends that she'd have no trouble getting permission.*  So what's at issue here is not the movie, or a difference of medical opinion, or the mother's right to say no.  While each of those elements plays a part in the dispute, the real issue, the controlling hidden agenda, is this:  Megan, having already said it was okay to go, doesn't want to have to back down, to be embarrassed in front of her friends, to admit to the higher authority of parental control.  Her hidden agenda is fear of losing face.  That's why she won't take no for an answer.

Suppose this hidden agenda had come up in the original discussion.  Would it have changed anything?  Let's see:

*"Mom, can I go to the movies Friday night?"*

*"I don't think so, Megan.  You've been sick all week and I think you should get as much rest as possible."*

*"But I feel fine.  And besides, I already told my friends I could go.  It never occurred to me you'd say no.  I go to the movies all the time."*

*"I know, but I still don't think it's a good idea.  You shouldn't have said you could go without checking first."*

*"I know, but I was sure you'd say yes.  Please, Mom, I'd be so embarrassed to have to tell them I can't go.  They've already made plans.  They're counting on my going.  Please?"*

*"You've just been so sick—"*

*"Please?  How about this.  I'll come straight home on Friday from school and take a nap.  Maybe Chris's dad can drive us and you could pick us up.  That way I won't have to walk in the cold.  Please?"*

*"All right. But you promise you'll take a nap and bundle up?"*

*"Promise. Don't worry. Thanks."*

In this case, the conflict was solved quickly because the hidden agenda came out in the open. Each person's needs and feelings could then be recognized and addressed. The mother was concerned about her child's health, and the child responded with a willingness to accept those feelings and incorporate them into a solution. This acceptance allowed the mother to be open and sensitive to her child's need to honor a commitment and save face.

You've got all sorts of emotional, practical, and psychological forces working overtime to create and maintain hidden agendas. How can you avoid them in the first place and uncover them if they've already developed?

- Present the idea of hidden agendas to your family. Let them know you're aware of this phenomenon and that you'll be making an effort to get to the bottom of any conflict. Ask them to do the same.

- Use Problem-Solving Sessions (described in the next section). The non-threatening nature of this approach encourages people to state their needs and feelings honestly, thus revealing issues that might otherwise remain underground.

- Develop lines you can use to steer a discussion towards what's truly at stake. You might try:

  *"What are we really arguing about here?"*

  *"Do you have the feeling that there's something else going on?"*

  *"This seems like such a silly thing to be fighting about. Maybe there's a deeper issue."*

  *"I think there may be something we're/you're/I'm feeling that hasn't come up yet in the discussion."*

  *"I can't believe we'd all get this upset about _____ " (fill in the blank) "unless there's something else going on."*

Be prepared to follow up these openers with I-messages and Active Listening. It wouldn't be fair to ask your folks to reveal deep feelings and then blast them for it.

■ *Gather intelligence.* The more you learn about your parents' lives, experiences, and values, the more accurately you can sniff out their hidden agendas. Don't jump to conclusions. You could be wrong.

■ *Be honest with yourself.* Why are you so invested in a certain position? Why is it so important to have a particular freedom? How come you get so upset by this and so hurt by that? Look for clues. What's really going on? Why did your emotions get so out of proportion to what actually happened?

You may not like certain feelings you find; they may make you confused, ashamed, or uncomfortable. But if you avoid them, they'll do their work secretly and destructively. They won't go away. If you identify them, no matter how weird or abnormal they seem, you'll keep in touch with your own hidden agendas, you'll bring more control to your life, and you'll avoid getting backed into positions that deep down you care nothing about.

Tuning in to hidden agendas will go a long way towards bringing up parents who are in touch with their feelings and yours. Clearer communication will lead to greater respect and trust—the foundations of your freedom and privileges. If you're going to have fights at home (and you will), at least have them over *real* issues, Up-Front-Out-in-the-Open *known* issues. Don't waste energy and agony on superficial skirmishes conned by hidden agendas into masquerading as worthy conflicts.

# PROBLEM-SOLVING SESSIONS

The trouble with most family conflicts is that someone wins and someone loses or, in some cases, everyone loses. Parents and kids quickly back themselves, or get backed into, opposing corners. The issue itself gets lost. The real issue becomes one of power and authority. We already know how loathe parents and teenagers are to give up claims to their power and rights.

No matter what the conflict, everyone loses when battle lines are drawn. It becomes either my way or your way, but not both. The funny thing is, even if you do get your way, you may be so upset by the fighting that you won't enjoy the fruits of your victory.

Problems are normal, natural, and unavoidable. They are an inevitable accompaniment to interlocking lives and feelings. There's nothing wrong with you or your parents just because you have conflicts. It's not the problem that does the damage. *It's how the problem does or doesn't get solved that does the damage.*

What you're going to have to do is bring up your parents to approach problems as creative challenges, brain-teasers, puzzles in which the "winning" solution is the one in which the feelings and needs of all are heard. It sounds impossible because you're so used to the other way, the someone-wins-and-someone-loses way. But it's not impossible! Let's jump right in and see how a Problem-Solving Session (or P.S.S.) can be used to solve an everyday conflict. Then we'll look at how and why it works.

## The Problem: Telephone Use

You spend hours on the phone every night. You talk to your friends, chat up the latest news, and, sometimes, do homework together. Your parents don't like having the phone tied up, and your younger sister is getting to the age where she's starting to make more and more calls. She's being a little brat, complaining to your folks that you're always on the phone and it's not "fay-aire." Your parents are beginning to mutter ominous warnings about "no more phone calls at night" and "all calls limited to ten minutes or less." You don't like the sound of that.

Before this becomes a big issue, you decide (a very smart move) to call a Problem-Solving Session. Since this is the first P.S.S. you've ever had in your family, you begin by explaining how it works. They're quite curious (and somewhat suspicious), so you carefully lay things out ahead of time. That way, they don't feel you're pulling a fast one.

Here goes....

*YOU* (courageously beginning): **You know how when we get into fights, it almost always turns out that one person wants it one way, and another wants it another way, and then it becomes who's going to get his way? So then one person wins and the other loses and everyone's still mad?**

YOUR FAMILY (cautiously responding): **Y-e-s-s-s-s....**

*YOU:* **Well, I've learned a new method that I want to show you for solving our problems so that no one ends up losing—everybody wins.**

DAD: **If this is just some trick for getting your way—**

*YOU:* **No, Dad, this isn't a trick at all. It's impossible for me to get my way unless it's okay with you and Mom and Sis. Just watch. It may seem strange at first, but after a while I bet you and Mom will want to use this method as much as me.**

DAD: **All right. How does it work?**

*YOU:* **Okay. There are six steps.**
**First, we *define* the problem.**
**Second, we *brainstorm* for solutions.**
**Third, we *discuss and evaluate* the solutions.**
**Fourth, we *agree to choose* the best solution to try.**
**Fifth, we take steps to *carry out* the solution.**
**And sixth, we *check up on* the solution to see how it's worked.**

YOUR FAMILY: **Wait a minute—**
**But I don't—**
**How's that going to—**

*YOU:* **You're all talking at once! Mom?**

MOM: **Isn't this going to take a lot of time?**

*YOU:* **Dad?**

DAD: **What happens when it's time to choose and we disagree? Aren't we right back to where we started?**

*YOU:* **Sis?**

SIS: **I don't get it. Can you explain it again?**

*YOU:* **Let's just try it. I'll explain as we go along. It's like learning the rules of a new game. It's a lot easier if you just start playing. Okay?**

YOUR FAMILY: **Okay.**

*YOU:* **Like I said, first, we *define* the problem. That way, we know we're all talking about the same thing. We define it by talking about our *feelings* and our *needs.* But you can't blame other people. You have to say, "I would like to use the car Friday night," as opposed to, "You won't let me have the car Friday night." See the difference? That way, we won't get everything off on the wrong foot by attacking people. That's really important. Here, I'll go first.**

**I'm upset about the problems we're having with my use of the telephone at night. I'd like to be able to talk without feeling I'm making everyone else mad at me. Okay, now it's Mom's turn.**

MOM: **I worry that your schoolwork may suffer from all that time spent on the phone. I feel like I should do something.**

*YOU:* **Dad?**

DAD: **People from work have told me that they've tried all night to reach me and the line's been busy. I'd like to feel that people who need to talk to me will be able to do just that.**

*YOU:* **Sis?**

SIS: **You don't ever let me use the phone. You act as if you own the whole—**

*YOU:* **Wait a minute. You're blaming me. Don't attack me, just say what you feel and want.**

SIS: **Okay, I'll try. All right. I think that you don't ever let me—**

*YOU:* **No, that's the same thing. Try again.**

SIS: **I want to be able to use the phone, too.**

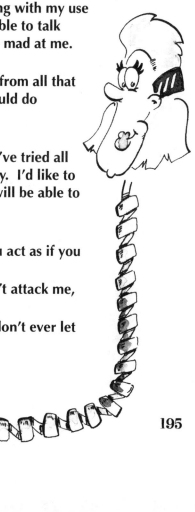

*YOU:* **There you go!  Great....  Now, let's summarize the problem according to what everyone's said.  I like to talk on the phone and feel that it's something I should be able to do without upsetting others.  Mom is worried about the effect on my schoolwork.  Dad wants to know that his friends and work people can get through.  Sis wants to be able to use the phone, too.  Does that sound right?**

YOUR FAMILY: **Sounds fine to me.  Now what?**

*YOU:* **Okay.  Now we go to step two, where we *brainstorm* for solutions.  That means we try to think up as many possibilities as we can, no matter how silly or far-out they seem.  We're looking for quantity here.  Even wild ideas may lead to a good solution.**
**The only rules are that you can't talk about the ideas now, and you can't criticize anyone else's ideas.  No discussion, no put-downs, just tons of ideas.  And someone should write them down.  Mom, can you?  All right.  Who's got ideas?  Sis?**

SIS: **Get a new phone just for me.**

DAD: **Now, cookie, we can't—**

*YOU:* **No discussion, Dad.  Remember?  Just brainstorm now.  Mom?**

MOM: **We could limit the time you can be on the phone each night.**

DAD: **No phone calls after eight o'clock.**

SIS: **Get a kid's phone.**

*YOU:* **Throw the phone out.**

DAD: **No more than ten minutes a call.**

MOM: **Get an unlisted number.**

*YOU:* **Get off the phone if Dad wants to call.**

DAD: **Yeah, but what if—**

*YOU:* **Can't discuss now.  Later we can, but not now.  How about letting Sis use the phone 'til 8:30, since she goes to bed earlier than me and then I could use it afterwards.**

SIS: **Why do I have to go to bed so early?**

*YOU:* **Sis!**

DAD: **We could get call-waiting.**

*YOU:* **Any other ideas? Mom?**

MOM: **We could link your phone use to your grades, maybe. If your grades fell we'd cut back on phone time.**

SIS: **Get a pay phone.**

DAD: **Write more letters.**

*YOU:* **Okay, anything else?**

YOUR FAMILY: **No.**

*YOU:* **All right, then. Now we're ready for step three. That's where we *discuss and evaluate* the ideas. Mom, can you read the list?**

MOM reads the list.

*YOU:* **Okay. Now let's discuss the ideas. Sis?**

SIS: **I think we should throw out "write letters." I don't like to write and if you need to know something right away you can't send someone a letter.**

*YOU:* **Any objections?**

MOM: **No, and while we're at it, let's eliminate "pay phone" and "throw the phone out."**

DAD: **And "unlisted number." How could anyone call us if they can't get our number?**

*YOU:* **Anyone mind if we throw those ideas out? I'd like to throw out the bad grades idea, too.**

MOM: **Why do you want to throw that out?**

*YOU:* **Look, Mom. How have my grades been?**

MOM: **Why, they're fine.**

*YOU:* **That's my point. I may spend a lot of time on the phone, but sometimes I'm doing my homework. When you say, "bad grades, no phone," I feel like I'm under a threat, you know, like this big sword is hanging over me. I think it's just a worry you have. If my grades fall,**

197

then we can talk about stopping the phone. But not now. Why worry about a problem that isn't even there?

DAD: **That's a good point.**

MOM: **Okay. I'll agree to drop my idea.**

YOU: **Whew. Thanks, Mom. Now—these ideas about getting a kids' phone or getting Sis a phone of her own. Who's going to pay for that? I sure don't have the money.**

SIS: **Me, neither.**

DAD: **Me, neither.**

SIS: **Oh, Dad, you have the money!**

DAD: **What I mean is, I don't think I should have to shell out money for another phone line. Especially now that the rates are so high. Maybe there are other ideas that are still better.**

YOU: **If Mom has dropped her worry about the phone and my grades, that leaves two problems: Sis being able to use the phone, and Dad's friends being able to call.
I don't think we need to limit calls or say this is when I can use the phone and you can't 'cause it would be silly if I wasn't using the phone to not let you use it. What if we combine some of the ideas like this: Sis has priority for using the phone up to 8:30 P.M.**

SIS: **What does that mean?**

YOU: **It means if you want to use it and I want to use it, you get first crack. So, anyway, Sis would get priority up to 8:30. If Mom or Dad wants to use the phone, we have to get off within five minutes. The last thing is, we should get call-waiting. That way, even if I'm talking, I can still answer the phone, and if it's for Dad, I'll get him or take a message and get off the phone within five minutes.
How does that sound? Sis?**

SIS: **Great. You mean, I get the phone all to myself until 8:30?**

*YOU:* **If you want to talk. I can still use it but I'll get off if you need it.**

SIS: **Wow!**

*YOU:* **Mom?**

MOM: **Sounds fine to me.**

*YOU:* **Dad?**

DAD: **I like it. I'm just wondering who's going to pay for call-waiting.**

*YOU:* **What if we split it? It's not that much, is it? I could put in a dollar or two a month and Sis could, too, and you and Mom would benefit so you could share, too.**

DAD: **Tell you what. I'm very pleased you're willing to share in the cost. It's not a lot, and I had considered call-waiting for us before this came up, so I would be willing to pay for all of it.**

*YOU:* **Gee, thanks, Dad!**

DAD: **You're welcome. So, are we done?**

*YOU:* **Just about. We just finished the *agree to choose* step. There are two steps left, and they're really important. We have to be sure that we've thought of everything to *carry out* the solution. You know—who does what. Let's write the solution down so we can be sure to remember what we decided and check up on it later. The only thing we have to do to carry it out is to get the call-waiting.**

MOM: **I'll call the phone company in the morning.**

DAD: **Mom'll call the phone company. Anything else?**

*YOU:* **The last step is to *check up on* the solution. You know, see how it's working out. We can't do that now, but at our next P.S.S. we'll see how things are going.
That's it, then. Let's set a time for our next meeting.**

Problem-Solving Sessions work!  Why do they work?

1. Many problems exist simply because no one bothers to solve them. A P.S.S. focuses attention on one problem until it's solved.

2. The steps give structure to the process.  They provide a sense of security and help guide you to a solution.

3. No one's on trial, no one's in the hot seat.

4. The process leads to creative solutions and compromises that might otherwise never be considered.

5. Only when *everyone* agrees to a solution is it carried out.  Nobody loses.  There are no votes, no majority rules.  It's a process of looking for places where you can agree.  People are much more likely to carry out a decision they helped to make than one imposed upon them.

6. A P.S.S. respects people's needs and feelings.

7. The process focuses on the future rather than the past, on solving rather than blaming.

8. P.S.S.'s work for practically any problem or conflict, before or after it has erupted.

9. The process builds good feeling and cooperation.  The family gains confidence in its ability to deal with dilemmas; problems are less likely to career out of control.

10. Aren't nine reasons enough?

Here are some tips to maximize the chances that Problem-Solving Sessions will work for you and your family:

1. Be sure to explain how it works ahead of time.  You don't want your family to feel conned or threatened by this new method.

2. Be patient.  Good things take time to nurture.

3. Be sure people follow the rules.  They are there to protect feelings.  No You-statements are allowed because they attack.  No judgments or discussion are allowed during the brainstorm because they inhibit people's contributions.  Who's going to risk giving an idea if someone else will label it "dumb"?

4. Set a regular time for your P.S.S.  Your family is busy.  If there's no regular slot, it could be hard to get everyone together.  If an emergency

comes up, you can always call a special P.S.S. If it's the regular P.S.S. and you don't have any P.'s to S., you can adjourn or go get a pizza.

A P.S.S should be fun. Don't use it as a gripe session; use it for constructive purposes. If an issue defies solving, table it until next time. You may get some good ideas in the meantime.

5. Don't meet for too long. People get restless, thinking gets fuzzy, and resistance can build. You might schedule the session so issues involving younger siblings get brought up first. They can be free to leave when you deal with problems directly involving you and your folks.

6. If someone with a key role in a conflict can't be there for a legitimate reason, try to re-schedule. If someone just can't be bothered, go ahead and solve the problem anyway. Democracy requires participation. If a family member won't participate, he or she loses the chance to have a say-so.

7. Be on guard against Silly Solutions, Absurd Approaches, and Ridiculous Resolves. In your desire to reach agreement (or to finish up in time for a TV show), you may accept a solution that's patently preposterous. Don't agree just so you can say you've solved the problem.

Be realistic; if you know your phone calls average an hour, don't pretend you can suddenly limit them to five minutes. If you don't have any money, don't agree to pay for a new phone line for yourself. Got it?

8. Some solutions will fall apart. Perhaps the problem was misidentified, the solution was unclear, the circumstances changed, or someone forgot to carry out a responsibility. Spend some time during each P.S.S. checking up on prior problems. If something has come unraveled, take a new look at it to figure out what went wrong.

9. There are no right or wrong solutions. What works for you and your family won't necessarily work for another family. A solution is right if everybody agrees on the chosen course of action.

10. Let a different family member lead the session each time. This will prevent any one person from becoming a Problem-Solving Prima Dominator.

Following are some objections, criticisms, and difficulties you might encounter while introducing Problem-Solving Sessions to your family. **DO NOT READ ABOUT THEM** unless you truly want to become a masterful troubleshooter.

**Objection #1:** *Takes too much time. How can we spend a half-hour every time a problem comes up?*

There's no question that P.S.S.'s take time. In the beginning, when you and your family are getting used to the method, it *will* take a lot of time. But to that you can say:

*"If our family isn't worth the time, what is?"*

*"Think of all the time we spend fighting, arguing, and sulking. Wouldn't you rather spend the time working together towards solving our problems?"*

*"The more we use P.S.S.'s, the less time each problem will take."*

*"With this strategy for attacking problems, our family will get more in tune with each other, we'll feel better, and the number of conflicts we have will diminish. In the long run, P.S.S.'s will actually save time because we'll have fewer run-ins."*

**Objection #2:** *Sounds tricky. You must have something up your sleeve. What makes you think a family that fights all the time is going to suddenly turn around and agree about things?*

People are naturally suspicious about new ideas and change. They like security; they'd almost prefer an *un*pleasant known to a pleasant *un*known. All you can do is acknowledge that this is a new approach and that you'll understand if people are wary or uncomfortable at first. Make your commitment strong, and people will feel your faith in the method.

There's nothing tricky about it; every step of the process is open and visible to all. Your parents have to be impressed by the fact that you are willing to sit down with them and work things out. In fact, if your traditional position has been one of open warfare, you have to admit they have a right to be a little suspicious and wonder what's up.

Come to think of it, you *do* have something up your sleeve: a desire to make life more pleasant for you and your family, and to put a stop to the destructive win/lose cycle of problem-"non-solving" that currently exists.

### Objection #3:

I've saved the biggest obstacle for last. It's so big, in fact, that it won't fit into one short title. It has to do with *power*.

Chances are good that your parents see themselves as the authorities in the family. (I'm sure you're an authority on that!) They reserve decision-making (or at least veto rights) for themselves.

**"We're not turning control of this family over to a child."**

**"We're not giving up our right to say what goes."**

They will feel threatened by Problem-Solving Sessions, as if they're going to lose their power. You're going to have to be on your toes to deal with this fear. In a way, they are losing power and, then again, they're not. They're going to *lose* the power they shouldn't have in the first place, and *gain* a new power they'd want to have if they could get out of their old mindsets.

You'll have to decide how to present these concepts. I'll lay out the ideas for you.

If your folks are most concerned about loss of power, explain to them that they're not losing power. They're gaining it. And so are you. It's the power that comes from increased trust and respect. No decision can be made unless everybody agrees. Your parents' values and feelings will find their way into a solution. Just because you and your siblings start to share in the decision-making process doesn't mean that your parents have lost power. Besides, if you all agree to a solution, the chances that you'll follow through are improved. Isn't that what your parents want? So how are they giving up any power? The biggest point to get across is that nothing happens unless *they* (and you, but *shhhh*) agree.

Another way to approach the issue is: What Other Choice Is There?

Your parents' ability to control you does decrease as you reach your teens. You spend more time away from home, and you are increasingly influenced by your friends, by school, by what you see in the world. What if your parents disapprove of your behavior? You're too old to pick up and put in a crib, you're too old to spank, and they darn well better not hit you. If they're

into power tripping, about all they have left in their arsenal is the ability to threaten and punish. No money, no party, no TV, no license, no this, no that. If you resist, they escalate the threat, intensify the punishment. Eventually they run out of options. But by then they have destroyed the relationship, and you've started to hate them, lie to them, do things out of spite, and all is lost. What power do they have in this mess?

The only real choice they have is to create a new balance of power in your relationship. Problem-Solving Sessions are a perfect structure for doing that.

You probably see the paradox here. In one sense, your parents do (and should) lose power as you get older and share in decision-making. But they only lose *cheap* power, *authoritarian* power, power that sets them up to win and you to lose. This is the power they may be used to, and this is why they may feel a loss. However, if power is defined as the ability to influence people and events, your parents will definitely gain power by giving you more respect and participation, by placing higher value on your feelings and rights as a human being, by giving you an equal voice in family issues. Their actions will increase your respect and affection for them, making you more likely to listen to their point of view.

These are some subtle notions here—possibly too subtle for your parents to understand. Nevertheless, if these issues come up, help your parents to see that what they lose in Bully Power they'll more than gain in Love Power.

# Chapter 6

# CURES FOR THE COMMON CONFLICT:

## A PROBLEM APPENDIX

$T$eenagers the world over share many of the same problems: arguments over what you can do and where you can go; parents who snoop into your life; bedtimes, allowances and curfews; parents who don't like your clothes, your hair, your makeup, your posture, your everything. The list goes on—school, homework, grades, bad attitude, bad manners, sex, drugs, rock 'n' roll, drinking, driving, and "Clean That Room!!!"

While thousands of households are fighting over these issues at this very moment, each household's conflict is unique. The specifics of each family and each argument will suggest the best route to a solution.

This section presents an array of common parent-teenager problems. Use it as a guide for your own thinking and problem-solving. You may find ideas here that will make your problems disappear faster than a batch of warm, fresh-baked chocolate-chip cookies left sitting on the kitchen table.

On the other hand, you may discover that none of these ideas addresses your particular family situation. If that's the case, improvise. Combine ideas, let your mind wander down paths of imagination and flexibility. Sooner or later, you'll hit upon the winning combination of tactics to meet your problem and your needs.

# TURF: WHO OWNS THIS PROBLEM, ANYWAY?

Ready to tackle a problem? Great. Before you do, though, take a moment to figure out who owns it.

Here's how. Imagine that your life is a piece of land. On that land you keep your needs, your feelings, your rights, your freedoms. From time to time, people are going to trespass on your land, violate your turf. They'll stomp all over your feelings, they'll squash your rights, block your freedoms, and ignore your needs. When that happens—when your turf is invaded—*you own the problem*. You own the problem because something is interfering with your needs as a human being. You're the one who is unhappy, worried, confused, upset, ignored, restricted.

Now let's say you go out for a walk and cut across someone else's life. You trample their rights, you crush their feelings, you step on their needs. But you're having a lovely walk. You don't have any problem. *They own the problem* because it's their turf you've invaded.

Looking homeward, suppose you turn your stereo up so loud your parents can't think straight. *They own the problem* because you're trespassing on their needs. They're the ones with the headache, the inability to concentrate, the churning stomach. You, meanwhile, are satisfying your interests, doing just what you want. You don't have any problem. Yet.

If your parents charge into your room, yank the stereo off the shelf, and announce that they're taking it away for a month, the problem now has a new owner. *You.* Congratulations! Now your desire to listen to music is blocked. Your needs are thwarted. Your parents gave you their problem. They no longer own it because the house is quiet, and their turf is not invaded anymore.

Of course, you might choose to take some retaliatory action. You could create a new problem for your parents to own. But that's not problem-solving. That's problem-shifting. Beware of solutions that just throw problems back and forth, where the satisfying of one person's needs results in the violation of another person's needs. The perfect solution is one which makes a problem

disappear totally—no one owns it anymore.  That's why Problem-Solving Sessions work so well.  The process incorporates everyone's needs and feelings into a solution.

If you can figure out who owns a problem, you'll have valuable clues to help find a solution.  The charts on the following two pages illustrate some possible problem-solving routes for times when you're the proud owner of a problem, and times when your parents own a problem.  The numbers point you towards the chapters in this book that describe each strategy.

**BEGIN HERE**

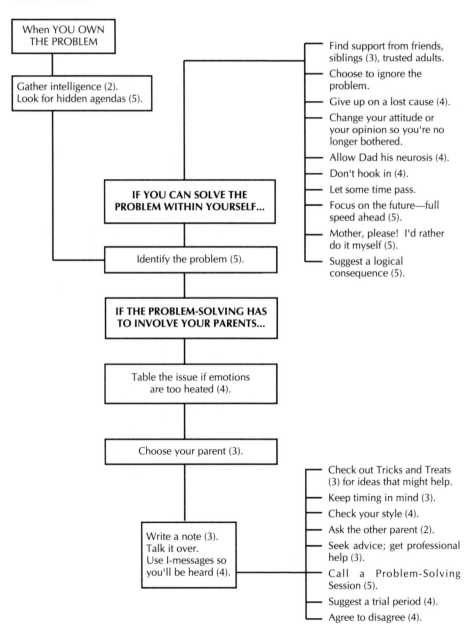

When YOU OWN THE PROBLEM

Gather intelligence (2).
Look for hidden agendas (5).

**IF YOU CAN SOLVE THE PROBLEM WITHIN YOURSELF...**

Identify the problem (5).

**IF THE PROBLEM-SOLVING HAS TO INVOLVE YOUR PARENTS...**

Table the issue if emotions are too heated (4).

Choose your parent (3).

Write a note (3).
Talk it over.
Use I-messages so you'll be heard (4).

Find support from friends, siblings (3), trusted adults.

Choose to ignore the problem.

Give up on a lost cause (4).

Change your attitude or your opinion so you're no longer bothered.

Allow Dad his neurosis (4).

Don't hook in (4).

Let some time pass.

Focus on the future—full speed ahead (5).

Mother, please! I'd rather do it myself (5).

Suggest a logical consequence (5).

Check out Tricks and Treats (3) for ideas that might help.

Keep timing in mind (3).

Check your style (4).

Ask the other parent (2).

Seek advice; get professional help (3).

Call a Problem-Solving Session (5).

Suggest a trial period (4).

Agree to disagree (4).

**209**

BRINGING UP
PARENTS

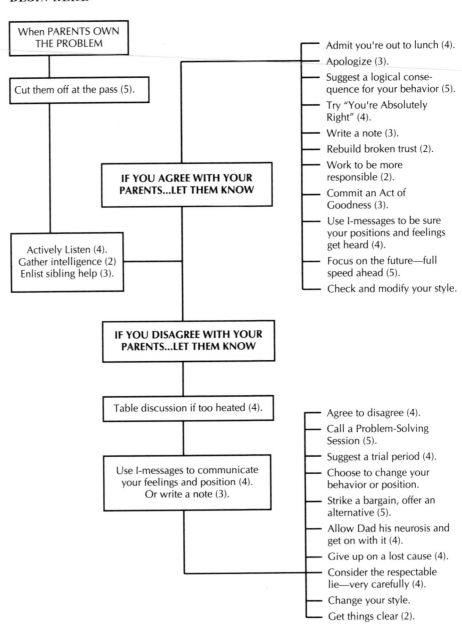

**BEGIN HERE**

When PARENTS OWN
THE PROBLEM

Cut them off at the pass (5).

IF YOU AGREE WITH YOUR
PARENTS...LET THEM KNOW

Actively Listen (4).
Gather intelligence (2)
Enlist sibling help (3).

Admit you're out to lunch (4).

Apologize (3).

Suggest a logical conse-
quence for your behavior (5).

Try "You're Absolutely
Right" (4).

Write a note (3).

Rebuild broken trust (2).

Work to be more
responsible (2).

Commit an Act of
Goodness (3).

Use I-messages to be sure
your positions and feelings
get heard (4).

Focus on the future—full
speed ahead (5).

Check and modify your style.

IF YOU DISAGREE WITH YOUR
PARENTS...LET THEM KNOW

Table discussion if too heated (4).

Use I-messages to communicate
your feelings and position (4).
Or write a note (3).

Agree to disagree (4).

Call a Problem-Solving
Session (5).

Suggest a trial period (4).

Choose to change your
behavior or position.

Strike a bargain, offer an
alternative (5).

Allow Dad his neurosis and
get on with it (4).

Give up on a lost cause (4).

Consider the respectable
lie—very carefully (4).

Change your style.

Get things clear (2).

210

# Problems of the Homegrown Variety

## Trials and Tribulations of Living Together

### The Issue Arena: Food/Mealtimes

| Problem | How You See It | How Your Parents See It |
|---|---|---|
| Different food likes and dislikes. | "Yicch. I can't stand this." | "You'll eat what you're served." |
| Sharing mealtimes. | "Why do we all have to eat together?" | "Mealtime is family time. We like to eat with our children." |
| The time of dinner. | "It's too early. Why can't I eat later?" | "I'm not running a restaurant. Either you eat when we do or you can go hungry." |
| Taking food out of the kitchen. | "I like to eat when I watch TV." | "No food is allowed outside of the kitchen. It'll bring ants." |
| Nutrition versus junk food. | "Quick. Help me! I'm having a Big Mac Attack." | "If you want a snack, there are some sunflower seeds in the cabinet." |
| Parents think you have lousy table manners. | "All they worry about is how I hold my fork." | "How can you go to other people's houses and expect to be invited back?" |
| | "There are more important things than where your elbows are." | "We're embarrassed to think that any child of ours would behave like that." |

## Be honest. Questions to ask yourself:

- Are you a junk food/soda fiend? Are your habits unhealthy (even though they taste good)?
- Do you leave a mess in the kitchen?
- Are you a finicky eater?
- Have mealtimes become yet another stage set for family bickering?

## Some things to consider:

- Separate the issues. Look for hidden agendas. Are you trying to avoid shared mealtimes for practical reasons (so you don't have to come home at 6:00) or because of something else (like the family fighting that occurs 'round the dining room table)?
- Have a P.S.S. Establish clear household policies for eating and meal-times. Examples:
  —If you clean up after yourself, you can help yourself to snacks.
  —If you give advance notice, the dinner hour can be changed.
  —If you don't want to eat, you don't have to, but you can't take food later.
- Make a list of "family-approved" menus that everyone likes.
- Make dinnertime special. Experiment with foreign cuisine. Have a dress-up fancy dinner. Invite interesting friends to join the family (but do check with your parents first to make sure that tonight isn't Clean-Out-the-Refrigerator-Mystery-Casserole-Night).
- Make a clear list of who does what when: setting the table, clearing, cooking, dishes, etc.
- Suggest a trial period for improving table manners. Identify the most sought-after etiquettes. Ask your parents not to remind you at the table in exchange for your greater efforts to remember for yourself.

## The Issue Arena:  Phone Use

| Problem | How You See It | How Your Parents See It |
|---|---|---|
| Parents think you spend too much time on the phone. | "No one else is using it." | "We don't like having the line tied up.  What if somebody's trying to reach us?" |
| | "We do homework together." | "The homework takes five minutes.  The gossip takes five hours." |
| | "Take away my phone and you take away my will to live." | "Your grades are going to suffer." |

## Be honest.  Questions to ask yourself:

- Are you a phone hog?
- Do you get off the phone when others need to use it?
- Are you doing poorly in school?  Is there any reason for your parents to be concerned?

## Some things to consider:

- Search out hidden agendas.  Is it *that* you're talking or *to whom* you're talking that bugs your parents?  Do your folks fear you're using the phone to do something you shouldn't?
- Consider getting a kids' phone line.
- Get call-waiting service.  Establish "priority hours" for who has first dibs at what times.
- Have a P.S.S. to deal with the specifics of the conflict.  (See pages 193–199 for a P.S.S. on precisely this problem.)

## The Issue Arena: Room Sharing

| Problem | How You See It | How Your Parents See It |
|---|---|---|
| You're unhappy about sharing a room. | "I don't have any privacy." | "Worse things can happen than having to share a room." |
| | "I can't have friends over." | "You can entertain in the family room." |
| | "All because of him, I have to go to bed earlier." | "There isn't a bedroom of your own to have, or we'd let you have it." |

## Be honest. Questions to ask yourself:

- Are you the only one who has to share, or is everyone in the house cramped for space?
- Millions of *whole families* live in one room! Given your family's size and finances, are you being reasonable in expecting a room of your own?

## Some things to consider:

- Assuming that the problem occurs because there *isn't* an empty bedroom lying around with your name on it, could you:
  —Partition your room for privacy?
  —Swap spaces with another sibling?
  —Set up a private space for yourself in an unlikely spot such as the basement, attic, or loft over the garage?
- Is your family in a position to consider moving to a larger house or building an addition?
- In nice weather, set up a tent or build a tree house for yourself.

## The Issue Arena:  Not Cleaning Up after Yourself

| Problem | How You See It | How Your Parents See It |
| --- | --- | --- |
| Making a mess wherever you go. | "I don't mind it." | "If you make the mess, you clean it up!" |
| Leaving things out. | "I forget.  Besides, I'll be coming back to it anyway." | "Someone will trip and get hurt." |
| Bad attitude towards cleaning up. | "If they don't like it, they can clean it up." | "We're not your maids." |

## Be honest.  Questions to ask yourself:

- Why don't you clean up after yourself?  Because you're forgetful? Spoiled?  Lazy?  Oblivious to chaos?
- Do you expect someone else to clean up for you?
- Is it fair for your mess to invade other people's space?

## Some things to consider:

- Designate a "mess hall" or workshop where it's okay to leave things out.
- Have a P.S.S.  Talk over your varying definitions of "mess."  Make sure that you know what you mean by the word.  Try to understand what everyone else means.
- Get with the program.  Clean up after yourself.  It's only fair.  How would you feel if someone left things strewn about your room?
- Propose a logical consequence for yourself if you continue to forget to clean up.

## The Issue Arena: Noise

| Problem | How You See It | How Your Parents See It |
|---|---|---|
| Parents complain about your noisiness. | "What? I can't hear you." | "It's TOO NOISY!!!" |
| Parents don't like your music. | "If they don't like it, they don't have to listen to it."* | "You call that music?!?" |

## Be honest. Questions to ask yourself:

- Are you a noise polluter? Do the neighbors think they've heard a sonic boom every time you turn on the stereo?
- Do your parents object to the noise itself, or to *when* you choose to make it?
- Have you cleaned out your ears lately? I said, HAVE YOU CLEANED OUT YOUR EARS LATELY???

## Some things to consider:

- Be quieter.
- Close your door.
- Use headphones.
- Wait 'til your folks leave the house to blast off the decibel charts.
- Offer to establish "quiet hours" in exchange for some "high volume" time.
- Soundproof your room. If you can't find actual builders' materials, you can use blankets, foam, carpeting, cork board, and the like to deaden sound. Think layers.
- Buy your folks ear plugs.
- Turn down the bass.
- Wait a few years. If it's really that noisy, you'll all begin to lose your hearing.

*I'm glad you said that. Keep it in mind next time your parents ask you to turn down the stereo.

## The Issue Arena: Cleanliness of Your Room

**Problem**

What else? Your parents think your room's a disaster.

**How You See It**

"It's my room. I should be able to keep it any way I want."

"They don't have to be in it if they don't like it."

**How Your Parents See It**

"No room in our house is going to look like a pig sty."

"You show no respect for your property."

## Be honest. Questions to ask yourself:

- Just how filthy is your room?
- Why is it such a mess? Because you know how much it bothers your folks? Because you don't have time to clean it? Because you don't have enough storage space?
- Do you share a room? Does your cohabitant mind its condition?
- Are you creating a health hazard?
- Do you rent your house or apartment? Is it reasonable that the landlord would object?
- Does your room smell?
- Are fuzzy mutant life forms growing in the corners?

## Some things to consider:

- Keep the door shut.
- Make a deal: Only "dead" messes allowed. No food, drink, or moldy, creepy, crawling creatures.
- Trade off your messy room in exchange for helping to clean other areas of the house.
- Have a P.S.S. to talk things through.
- Eliminate any effects your disorder may have on other people or spaces. Then try to get your parents to agree to consider your room a private space.

217

- Deal with any practical reasons for the mess: not enough storage space, room too small, friends come over and leave destruction in their wake.
- Set aside one ritualized time each week to blitz through your room with a quick clean-up.
- Establish a "throw-place" under your bed, in a trunk, or in the closet to confine your disorder to one or two out-of-sight, out-of-mind locations.
- Hire someone to clean up after you. (Siblings make excellent hired hands.)

## The Issue Arena: Bathroom Habits

| Problem | How You See It | How Your Parents See It |
|---|---|---|
| Parents complain about how long you take. | "Beauty takes time." | "Others need to use the bathroom, too." |
| Parents complain about the mess you leave. | "They're so compulsive about keeping everything neat and clean." | "Don't leave your towels on the floor." |
| | | "Clean the tub out after yourself." |
| | | "Put the seat up!" |
| | | "Don't forget to flush." |
| Toothpaste techniques. | "With everything they have to worry about, can't they give up on this one?" | "Roll the tube up as you use it!" |
| | | "Put the cap back on after you brush!" |

## Be honest. Questions to ask yourself:

- Do you infringe on other people's rights?
- Do you take much longer than everyone else?
- Are you a slob?

## Some things to consider:

- For toothpaste traumas, buy pumps or tubes with flip-up caps.  Or allow Dad his neurosis and roll the tube up.  Or buy your own tube and squeeze it any way you like.
- Boys: Put that seat up! And down when you're done! And close the lid! How would *you* like a wet behind?
- Does your bathroom need extra towel racks or a hamper?
- How about scheduling bathroom times based on:
  —who gets up first?
  —when people have to leave the house?
  —how much time they like to spend?
- Is there another bathroom in the house you could use, even if it's not as close to your bedroom?
- Do your reading and "other business" elsewhere.  Reserve your bathroom time for those activities that can only be done there.

## The Issue Arena:  Chores

| Problem | How You See It | How Your Parents See It |
|---|---|---|
| Parents nag you about doing chores. | "I wish they'd lighten up." | "If you did your chores, we wouldn't have to nag." |
| Uneven work loads. | "Why do I have to do more than them?" | "You can't compare. They're younger than you." |
| Finding time to do your jobs. | "I'm too busy." | "If you didn't goof off so much, you'd have the time." |
| Arguments about being paid for work. | "If I didn't do it, you'd have to pay someone else." | "You're a part of this family.  We don't get paid for our household responsibilities.  Neither do you." |

## Be honest. Questions to ask yourself:

- Do you forget to do your chores?
- Why should you be paid for contributing to family needs?
- If your siblings do less, is there a valid reason? Are they younger? Do they have schoolwork or other responsibilities that take away their time? Do they have physical limitations?

## Some things to consider:

- Make a clear list of your chores. Be sure you and your parents know what's expected.
- Establish a schedule for doing your jobs. Stick to it. You'll be less likely to forget.
- To stop parental nagging, do your jobs on time.
- Hire a sibling or swap days if you're not going to be able to do your chores.
- Ask your parents if they'd be willing to make a list of additional jobs you could do to earn extra money.

## The Issue Arena: Fighting with Siblings

| Problem | How You See It | How Your Parents See It |
|---|---|---|
| Fighting and needling one another. | "I hate them." | "I won't have you talking like that to one another." |
| | "She asks for it." | "Ignore her and act your age. She's five years younger than you." |
| | "We're just kidding around." | "Someone's going to get hurt." |
| | "It's not my fault. She started it." | "I don't care whose fault it is. This constant squabbling has got to stop." |

## Be honest. Questions to ask yourself:

- Why do you fight? Boredom? Habit? Taking something out on a convenient sibling?
- Do you treat your siblings the same way you hate your parents to treat you?
- What's your hidden agenda? Are you on a power trip? Are you jealous? Getting back at your parents?

## Some things to consider:

- Convince your parents that it's in everyone's best interests to allow you and your siblings to solve your own problems.
- Find out how your siblings feel. Do they take seriously what you take as teasing?
- Discover specific conflict areas and problem-solve them.

## The Issue Arena: Money

| Problem | How You See It | How Your Parents See It |
|---|---|---|
| Parents don't give you an allowance. | "It's my right to have an allowance." | "If you want money, go out and earn it." |
| Allowance is too small. | "I need more money." | "You get more than enough for someone your age." |
| Parents use allowance as a threat to get their way. | "It's not fair." | "It works, doesn't it?" |
| Parents don't like the way you spend money. | "It's my business how I spend my money." | "We're not giving you more money, since you'd only spend it on more junk." |
| Parents think you're spoiled and wasteful with money. | "I do value money. I just spend it in ways they don't like." | "You have no appreciation for the value of a dollar. Why, when I was your age...." |

## Be honest.  Questions to ask yourself:

- You want to get money each week just for belonging to your family. Do you participate in family chores each week because you belong to the family?
- We'd all like more money.  Is your allowance fair (even if you wish it were more) in terms of your family's finances, your needs, the number of other children, or unusual expenses in the household?

## Some things to consider:

- Kids cannot realistically be expected to support themselves.  They should receive an allowance that has nothing to do with chores or discipline.
- You receive an allowance because you belong to your family.  You do chores because you belong to your family.
- If you don't get an allowance, talk it over with your folks.  Be realistic about your expectations.  Find out why they aren't giving you one.  Is it because they don't have the money?  Because they think you're spoiled? Because they don't believe in giving allowances?
- Make a serious budget to show your monetary needs.  Go over it with your parents.  This might induce them to raise your allowance.
- If your folks forget to give you your allowance, remind them ahead of time.  Offer to go to the bank for them.  Send a reminder note. Get your allowance monthly instead of weekly.  Tell them you'll take a check.
- Need more money?  Get a job.  Ask your parents to make a list of extra chores you could do to earn bigger bucks.
- If your parents use your allowance as a discipline weapon, ask yourself if you give them other choices.  Do they use the threat of no allowance as a last resort, or as a first resort?  Suggest other consequences for your actions besides allowance withholding.

# It's My Life

## Problems Involving Values, Taste, Judgment and the Social You

### The Issue Arena: Peers: Choice of Friends

| Problem | How You See It | How Your Parents See It |
|---|---|---|
| Parents don't approve of your friends. | "Fine. They don't have to spend any time with them." | "We don't like the crowd you're hanging out with." |
| Parents think you spend too much time with your friends. | "I like being with my friends. That's what I care about most." | "There's more to life than friends. Like your school-work, for instance." |
| Parents think you're too easily influenced by your peer group. | "I think they'd rather blame my friends than me. But I make my own choices." | "If your friends say 'jump,' you jump. Why don't you think for yourself?" |

## Be honest. Questions to ask yourself:

- Are your folks just being parents, or is there a basis for their feelings?
- Are you hanging out with a bunch of losers to get back at your folks?
- Do you have trouble making friends? Do you hang out with this crowd because you like them or because they like you?
- When's the last time you made a new friend?
- Have you been getting into trouble with these friends?

## Some things to consider:

- What, specifically, do your parents object to in your friends? Use that information to seek hidden agendas and to problem-solve.

- If your parents trusted you, they wouldn't be worried about your friends. Where has the trust broken down? What are they afraid your friends will make you do?

- If your parents feel you spend too much time with friends, they probably feel you're not spending enough time doing something else. What? Reassure them on the something else, and they may back off. A trial period could be used here.

- Don't stick with a crowd you don't like just because it's there, or because your parents are against it. Make your own decisions.

- Tell your folks how you feel when they knock your friends. Use I-messages. Enlighten them as to the importance of peer groups to adolescents. They may have forgotten how important their friends were to them.

## The Issue Arena: Boyfriends/Girlfriends

| Problem | How You See It | How Your Parents See It |
|---|---|---|
| Parents think you're too young to have a boyfriend/girlfriend. | "We're not doing anything, if that's what they're worried about." | "You shouldn't get so serious about one person at your age. You don't know what love is about yet." |
| Parents think you and your boyfriend/girlfriend spend too much time together. | "It's my life. We wouldn't spend a lot of time together if we didn't enjoy it." | "You should get to know lots of different people." |
| Parents don't approve of your boyfriend/girlfriend. | "It's none of their business." | "We think you're making a big mistake, and we're just trying to prevent it." |

## Be honest.  Questions to ask yourself:

- Just how young are you?  And just how serious are you?
- Has this relationship caused you to tune out the rest of the world?
- Has this relationship done any damage to other areas of your life? School?  Friendships?
- Are you comfortable with groups of people?  Do you see other friends?
- Could you be retreating from social situations through this relationship?
- Are you going out with someone mainly to shock your parents?
- Are there any valid reasons for them to object to your love-choice?
- Are you in a relationship that you don't know how to end?

## Some things to consider:

- Find those hidden agendas.  What do your folks fear?  Sexual activity? The loss of your love?  That their baby's growing up?  That you're not paying attention to other responsibilities?  The problem can't be addressed until you know what it is.
- While teenage love is a wonderful condition, be aware that the teenager in love often comes across as someone missing a few marbles.  Public relations is important here.  Your parents might back off if you can convince them that you still look both ways before crossing the street.
- If your parents worry that you're limiting your social horizons, how about being with your boyfriend/girlfriend in larger groups?  Go out with other couples.
- If your friend is as wonderful as you feel, let your parents get to know him or her.  They might turn around and be delighted that you're in the company of such a good influence.  Emphasize your "partner's" academic success, excellent family background, and horror of drugs. The day could come when your parents beg you to spend more time together.

## The Issue Arena:  Dating

| Problem | How You See It | How Your Parents See It |
|---|---|---|
| Parents won't let you date. | "They're such jerks. Everyone dates.  What are they afraid of?" | "You're too young.  You'll get in over your head." |
| Parents don't want you to go steady. | "But I'm in love.  Besides, everyone goes steady." | "You should spend more time with other people." |
| Parents insist on meeting your dates. | "Emmm-barrassing!" | "We want to know who you go out with." |

## Be honest.  Questions to ask yourself:

- Are you dating because you want to or because it's the thing to do?
- Do you ever feel like you're moving too fast?
- Do you ever feel pressured to date or go steady?

## Some things to consider:

- Look for hidden agendas in your parents' feelings.  What are they worried about?  Sexual activity?  Peer pressure?  Schoolwork?  Drinking?  Drugs?  Did any of your siblings get into trouble by dating?  Are you the "baby" in the family?  The oldest?  Are your parents unable to "let go"?
- Keep communication open.  Trust is a big item in this issue arena.
- Reassure your parents that you love them and know they exist.
- Consider double or triple dating.  It might ease things for both you and your parents.
- Let your folks meet your date.  Unless you have something to hide, your parents might be less uptight if they know who you're out with.  Don't be embarrassed; your date has parents, too.
- Get home on time.  If you're late on a date, parents assume it's because you're doing something you shouldn't and have lost track of time.  So do it earlier and spare your folks the worry.

## The Issue Arena:  Parties

| Problem | How You See It | How Your Parents See It |
|---|---|---|
| Parents won't let you go to parties. | "They never let me do anything." | "We know what goes on at these parties." |
| | "If I can't go to parties, I'll be a social outcast." | "You can have a party at home if you want." |

## Be honest.  Questions to ask yourself:

- Do your parents have cause for concern?
- Have you ever come home from a party late, drunk, or high on drugs?
- Have houses been trashed by parties that you or your friends have attended?
- Do you try to shock your parents by telling them things that go on that you know will upset them?

## Some things to consider:

- Build trust.  Show that you're your own boss and can withstand peer pressure.
- Gather intelligence.  Find your parents' specific concerns.  Can they be addressed through a compromise, a trial period, a promise?
- Encourage your parents to talk to the party's "host parents."
- Problem-solve specific concerns.  Flexibility in curfews, transportation arrangements, and who you go with can be valuable chips at the bargaining table.

## The Issue Arena: Clothes/Grooming/Appearance

| Problem | How You See It | How Your Parents See It |
|---|---|---|
| Parents object to your:<br>— clothes<br>— hair<br>— posture<br>— hygiene<br>— sloppiness<br>— makeup | "They're always after me about something."<br><br>"It's my life. I should be able to look the way I want to."<br><br>"I don't tell them how to dress. It's none of their business how I look." | "You look like a _____."<br><br>"No child of mine is going out looking like that!"<br><br>"I'm embarrassed to be seen anywhere with you." |

## Be honest. Questions to ask yourself:

- Are you a fright for sore eyes?
- Are you dressing to your own taste or to shock your parents?
- Just what color pink is your hair?
- Do your teeth really look green and fuzzy?

## Some things to consider:

- Gather intelligence. Get your parents to remember the fashions and fads that their parents objected to. Depersonalize the conflict. It's not you versus your parents; it's the tastes of one generation versus the tastes of another.
- Look for compromise areas. In your world (school, parties, out with friends) you'll dress as you wish and your parents will agree to lay off. In your parents' world (the office, restaurants, out in public with them) you'll tone things down a bit. (You know, like only one earring per nostril.)

- Pay for your own clothes, or at least the most outlandish ones. If your parents weren't forking over the dough, they might object less to your spike collars.
- Strike bargains. You'll wash the purple dye out of your hair if they ease off on your leather jeans. That sort of thing.
- Find out your parents' specific objections. Is it your shirt or the fact that you tie it up to expose your bountifully bare belly? If it's the naked navel that's driving them bananas, wait until you leave the house before exposing your midsection. (Beware of hidden agendas: your parents may just be jealous that you've got a stomach worthy of such display.)
- Talk the issue through. Use I-messages to explain how you feel when they criticize your appearance; discuss the concept of being your own person, developing your own image. Live and let live.
- Phew. Take a bath.
- Blecch. Change your socks before they begin to crawl by themselves.

# Home of the Whoppers

## Drinking, Driving, Drugs, Child Abuse, and Sex

### The Issue Arena: Drinking

| Problem | How You See It | How Your Parents See It |
|---|---|---|
| Parents forbid you to drink. | "That's not fair. They drink." | "You're much too young to be drinking. And it's illegal." |
| Parents worry that you drink too much. | "My parents would think one molecule is too much to drink." | "An occasional sip of wine with us is one thing. But we don't approve of your going over to friends' houses and drinking. Where are their parents, anyway?" |
| Parents won't let you drive with friends who have been drinking.* | "I wouldn't go with them if they were really drunk or anything." | "We don't want you cruising around in cars, and that's final. It's too dangerous. You can call us to come and get you." |

## Be honest. Questions to ask yourself:

- Do you drink to impress your friends?
- Do you go out of your way to find opportunities to drink?
- Do you even like the taste?
- Have you ever gotten sick or thrown up from drinking?
- Have you ever felt out of control or unable to stop drinking?
- Do you usually get drunk when you drink?

*Good for them.

- Do things happen when you've been drinking that you can't remember afterwards?
- Has a friend or relative ever expressed concern about your drinking?
- Teenage alcoholism is a huge problem. It's in the nature of being an alcoholic not to admit it. How much do you drink? Have you ever wondered if you have a drinking problem? If you have, you do. If you haven't, you still may.

## Some things to consider:

There are no easy answers where teenage drinking is concerned. Teenage drinking is a national problem, with adolescents more likely than any other age group to be in an alcohol-related automobile accident. Yet kids believe they're immortal and it's always someone else who'll be killed. Unfortunately, that's what all the "someone elses" thought, too, while they were still alive to think.

As with drugs, the degree to which drinking could be harmful for you will have to do with who you are, why you drink, when you drink, how much you drink, where and with whom you drink, and how your life is going.

Dealing with your parents over the issue of drinking is going to be a lot easier if you have their trust. Their belief in your good judgment, independence, and responsibility will go a long way towards allowing you to navigate safely in the alcoholic waters of teenage society.

If you suspect you do have a drinking problem, can you:

- Talk it over with your folks?
- Talk it over with a trusted doctor, school counselor, teacher, or friend?
- Connect with an alcohol abuse program?
- Attend an A.A. (Alcoholics Anonymous) meeting? Do it now! Look in the phone book under "Alcoholics Anonymous."

## Drinking and Driving

It's not easy to announce to your friends, "Hey, let me out. You're too drunk to drive. I'm not gonna get myself killed," or to prevent someone who's drunk from getting in the car in the first place. But you have to do it because you're clearly your own, strong person who puts a higher value on your life and your friends' lives than a little flak. Good for you. You'll live not to regret it.

## Some other ideas for dealing with cars and drinking:

- Make a pact with your friends. Get everyone behind the notion of staying alive. Join or start a chapter of S.A.D.D.—Students Against Drunk Driving. Get peer pressure on your side.
- Use the "designated driver" system.
- Make contracts with your parents. Get your friends to do the same. Here's how a contract works:
  —If you're out with a group and the driver drinks, a parent will be called to do the driving.
  —The parent must agree to ask no questions at the time, make no comments, give no lectures, do no scolding, indulge in no yelling— just provide friendly, safe chauffeur service.
  —The situation can be discussed, but not until the next day.
  This doesn't mean it's just grand for you to drink whenever you want. It does mean that lives and safety come first.
- Spend the night. That way, no one has to drive.
- Call a taxi.
- Pool your money with friends and hire a driver (an older sibling, a reliable friend).
- Rent a limo.

## The Issue Arena:  Driving

| Problem | How You See It | How Your Parents See It |
|---|---|---|
| Parents won't let you drive with friends. | "How do they expect me to get anywhere?" | "We don't want you cruising around with inexperienced drivers." |
| Parents won't let you drive. | "It's my right to get a license at 16." | "You're too careless and aggressive." |
| Parents don't approve of your driving attitudes. | "They should talk." | "Driving is not a game. It's a huge responsibility." |
| Conflicts over borrowing the car. | "I need the car Friday night." | "We need the car Friday night." |

## Be honest.  Questions to ask yourself:

- Why do your parents feel the way they do?
- Have you or your friends had accidents?  Tickets?  Close calls?
- Has there been drinking and driving?
- Are you a show-off in a car?

## Some things to consider:

- Your parents won't back away from their concerns.  They are legitimate ones.  Only your super-responsibility will work towards a solution agreeable to all.  If you're a reckless or absent-minded person, you shouldn't drive.
- Let your parents meet those friends with whom you want to drive. Help your folks to build some trust in them.
- Make a list of rules and conditions to govern your driving and your friends' driving that will satisfy your needs and acknowledge your parents' concerns.

■ Recognize that the life-and-death nature of this issue means your parents are likely to stick to their guns. Ranting and raving will show immaturity, which is exactly what they feel shouldn't be behind the wheel of a car. Therefore, deal with the problem by demonstrating your wisdom, good judgment, and willingness to be realistic about the dangers involved.

Remember, this is an area where you can't afford a mistake. It could be the last one you'd ever make.

## The Issue Arena: Drugs

| Problems | How You See It | How Your Parents See It |
|---|---|---|
| Parents search your room and belongings for drugs. | "They have no right to go through my things." | "For something as dangerous as drugs, we'll search your room if we have to." |
| Parents forbid you to see friends who use drugs. | "They can't stop me. I'll see whoever I want." | "We don't want you influenced by these kinds of kids." |
| Parents worry that you use drugs. | "I've told them a million times I've never taken a drug in my life." | "We can't always trust you. How can we be sure you're telling the truth?" |

## Some things to consider:

If you don't use drugs, why are your parents so suspicious? Do you hang out with drug users? Are you spacey, unmotivated, or depressed? Have your grades taken a sudden dive? What are your parents misinterpreting?

Find out. Talk to them. There's got to be a trust breakdown if they search your room or won't accept your word. Reassure them of your good judgment and self-discipline. Ask a sibling or close friend to intervene on your behalf.

If you have used drugs, I'm not going to pat you on the back and say, "Go right ahead." But I'm not going to press the panic button, either. I'm not going to call you a rotten kid, or tell you that your whole life is going to be ruined because you tried marijuana. Obviously, there are adults who tried

drugs when they were young, put them aside, and grew up to lead happy, healthy, responsible lives.

The danger with taking drugs is this: It's a game of Russian roulette. Every time you do it, you place yourself at risk. Maybe you'll get away with it a few times, but the odds are against you. One chamber always has a bullet in it.

Let's look at some of these risks.

Adolescence can be a time of pain and vulnerability. Growing hurts. When you're hurting, it's natural to want to make the pain stop. But if you take drugs to deaden your feelings, to get outside of yourself, to fit in, to feel comfortable socially, you don't grow. You don't learn how to cope with life. If you go for the quick fix, the hilarity, the false security, your problem may temporarily disappear. Until you're straight again. A destructive cycle is in gear. Only now you've added another problem: drugs.

Think of a skill you've learned—skiing, skate boarding, playing the guitar. Remember when you were learning? All the falls, mistakes, embarrassments, frustrations? But you kept going. You faced the challenges, kept practicing, figured out what you were doing wrong. Now suppose that every time you had run into trouble, you had turned to drugs (and yes, alcohol is a drug, too). You might have forgotten your problem for a moment, but you would never have learned to conquer the obstacle.

Well, life is a skill, too. Learning how to live a good life takes a lot of practice. It takes a lot of tumbles and mistakes and embarrassments before you can learn to ride the waves, smooth the bumps, stay in the saddle, weather the storms (to mix a few metaphors). On an emotional and practical level, this is the greatest danger drug use poses to teenagers: It undermines their ability to learn the skills of life. In fact, if you've ever talked to kids who got into trouble with drugs and alcohol, they'll tell you that they stopped growing emotionally at whatever age they first started substituting drugs for life.

The "rushin'" roulette of drug use poses other hazards. Some drugs can kill you. You've probably read newspaper stories about people who have died this way. For instance, cocaine can cause respiratory failure. It only takes one time. Just because it doesn't happen the first time doesn't mean it won't happen the third or fifth or tenth time.

Other drugs can be impure or poisoned. You never know what you're getting—I mean, it's not as though drugs come with the Good Housekeeping Seal of Approval. You can also overdose on drugs. Every year, many teenagers

die from alcohol poisoning. They drink alcohol faster than their bodies can process it, and it kills them.

Sometimes, death from drugs or alcohol occurs indirectly. You have a bad trip. You panic. You think you can fly. You jump out a window. Splat.

You get drunk, you hop into a car, you drive into a tree.

You share a needle. You get AIDS.

Drugs and alcohol can also impair your judgment. You take risks and do things you wouldn't otherwise do if you were straight or sober. You try to swim across a lake; you practice unsafe sex; you get into a fight; you pull a daredevil stunt. If you're lucky, you might get away with it. If not, you might end up pregnant. Or crippled. Or humiliated. Or in jail. Or infected with AIDS. Or dead.

If you have a problem with drugs or alcohol, you either can or can't talk to your parents about it, and you either admit to having a problem or you don't. If you know you have a problem, talk to your folks, your doctor, your school counselor, a trusted teacher, friend, or adult. You're going to have to discover and deal with those elements of your life, emotions, and chemistry that are causing you to turn to drugs.

If you're not admitting to a problem, ask yourself a few questions:

- Are you doing more drugs now than you used to? Drinking more?
- Do you keep breaking promises to yourself about stopping or cutting down?
- Have limits you once placed on yourself disappeared? Example: "Only on weekends." "Never in school." "I'll never buy it." "No hard stuff."
- Have you lost any friends because of your drug or alcohol use?
- Do you feel tired, lazy, unmotivated, hopeless?
- Are you unhappy or depressed a lot?
- Do you feel guilty?
- Is your life in a rut? Have you done or learned anything new lately?
- Are your grades worse than before?
- What are you hiding from? What pain are you trying to avoid?
- Do you spend more time than ever before with people who drink and do drugs?

- Are you stealing to get money for drugs or alcohol?
- Are you fighting with your family more often?

If these questions ring familiar bells, you've probably got a serious problem. The biggest hurdle is admitting to it. Once you do that, help can be found. If you can't talk to your parents, talk to someone else you trust. Call a hotline, go to a community mental health center, consult with a doctor, a teacher, a school counselor, a therapist. Locate a substance-abuse program. Look in the phone book under "Alcoholics Anonymous" or "Narcotics Anonymous." These are support groups for people with a desire to stop drinking or taking drugs. You'll find people there who care, who understand, who have been where you are now. Be sure the person you talk to knows you want help.

Hang on, don't let go, don't let anyone tell you the problem will go away by itself. You'll find a million reasons to convince yourself that you don't have a problem, that everything will be fine if only this and if only that and you'll stop when school starts or when you get a car or when you go away to camp. Don't believe it. An addicted person can't be trusted to do much other than deceive himself or herself. But pretending won't make the problem go away. It will only make it worse.

Having said all this, I think you should get...high.

That's right. Get high. On life. The greatest highs are the natural ones. The ones that come from love, nature, beauty, creativity, knowledge, growth. Go after the highs that come from a job well done, from friendship, from giving. Get the adrenalin flowing, the endorphins pumping. Run, sing, fly. Open your heart to someone. Let someone else into yours. The greatest high you can get will never come from drugs. It will come from you.

## The Issue Arena:  Child Abuse

| Problem | How You See It | How Your Parents See It |
|---|---|---|
| Parents are alcohol or drug abusers. | "Maybe if I weren't such a rotten kid, he wouldn't drink." | "If I weren't under so much stress, I wouldn't have to drink." |
| | "I think my mother's an alcoholic." | "Just because I like a few drinks now and then doesn't mean I'm an alcoholic.  Besides, I can stop any time I want to." |
| Parents abuse you emotionally. | "Our family's a mess. Everyone lies and fights and pretends we don't have problems." | "Every family has its ups and downs.  My drinking has nothing to do with it. If they'd just stop bugging me...." |
| | "It must be my fault.  If I weren't such a bad kid, they wouldn't say the things they do." | "A little criticism never hurt anyone." |
| Parents hit you or beat you. | "I'm scared.  I don't know what to do." | "Kids need discipline." |
| | "He doesn't mean it.  He's always sorry afterwards." | "Okay.  Maybe I do lose my temper, but so did my father.  And I turned out all right, didn't I?" |
| Parents abuse you sexually. | "Nobody would ever believe me." | "I'm not hurting anyone. I love her.  It's love." |
| | "I'm too ashamed to say anything." | "I can't help myself. I have certain needs." |

## Some things to consider:

If your parents have a drinking or drug problem, *it is not your fault*. Their behavior is not the result of anything you do or don't do. It is the result of their own issues and/or disease. If their problem relates to abuse that you suffer (i.e., your parent gets drunk and hits you, or leaves you unattended and without food or money), you must first protect yourself from the abuse.

You cannot make someone else stop drinking or taking drugs. Only they can make themselves stop. But there are several things you can do to help yourself:

1. Contact ALATEEN. This is a support group for teenagers whose lives are affected by someone's drinking. Going to ALATEEN meetings can help you to understand the situation better and lead a happier life.

    AL-ANON is another support group which serves the same purpose. While AL-ANON is not specifically for teenagers, many teens attend and benefit from it. These groups should be listed in the phone book.

2. Your school may have a drug and alcohol education program. Talk to teachers and school counselors who participate in it. They understand what you are facing and will be able to help. They may steer you into counseling, put you in contact with ALATEEN, or propose other approaches, such as an intervention with the parent who drinks.

## If You Are Being (or Have Been) Abused....

First, *it is not your fault. It is never your fault.* Even if you have been "bad." You may deserve a lecture, a logical consequence, a loss of trust. But you never deserve to be tormented emotionally or beaten.

Physical child abuse is immoral and illegal. It does not teach children to behave. It teaches them to hate, to fear, and to be violent themselves. ("Maybe I do lose my temper, but so did my father....")

Abuse is not always physical. Children need love and attention to grow. Parents who neglect their children, who do not feed or clothe or care for them, are guilty of child abuse. Parents can also use words and guilt as weapons. Parents who regularly say things that hurt and demean their children are guilty of child abuse.

*Being the victim of sexual abuse is never the fault of the child.* Nobody has the right to touch you sexually, to force or manipulate you into sexual activity, or to involve you in sexual activity when you are too young to understand it.

If you are being (or have been) abused, you must get help. The abuse must stop. You are probably afraid, angry, and unsure what to do. You may have been threatened that you or someone you love will be harmed if you tell. You and someone you love are already being harmed. The harm will be far greater if you *don't* tell.

Talk to an adult you trust: your teacher, school counselor, coach, neighbor, doctor, school nurse, scout leader, rabbi, minister, priest. Talk to a relative you trust. Talk to your other parent. Most adults will respond immediately with love, understanding, and help. Occasionally, an adult will ignore, deny, or disbelieve what you tell him or her. This can happen because of his or her own involvement in the situation. For example, your mother may not want to believe that you have been sexually abused by your father because he is also *her* husband. Or a parent may fear financial ruin or public humiliation if the fact gets out. That is not *your* problem. Your problem is protecting yourself (and possibly your siblings as well). The abuse must stop.

If you are being (or have been) abused, you can also go to the police. Go to a community health clinic. Or a legal aid office. Look in the phone book under "Child Abuse." There should be a toll-free hotline you can call. If no number is listed, call the operator or directory assistance and ask for the number.

No kid should be abused. Including you.

## The Issue Arena:  Sexual Values/Conduct/Activity/Identity

| Problem | How You See It | How Your Parents See It |
|---|---|---|
| Parents are nosy about your sex life. | "It's none of their business." | "We have a right to know about our child's sex life." |
| Parents disapprove of all premarital sexual activity. | "They're such prudes. I bet I was an immaculate conception baby." | "Sex should be part of marriage." |
| Parents restrict you from situations that might lead to sexual pressure or temptation. | "If I want to have sex, there's nothing they can do to stop me." | "We just don't want you to get into any situations you're not ready for. Besides, the risk of getting AIDS is too great." |
| Parents pressure you to date. | "They make me feel like something's wrong with me because I don't have a boyfriend/girlfriend." | "You should get experience while you're young. Sow some wild oats." |
| Parents won't talk about sex. | "They get so embarrassed. I wish they wouldn't, because I don't know any other adults I can talk to." | "We're just not comfortable talking about these things.  We bought you a book.  Read it." |
| Parents won't accept or acknowledge your sexual identity. | "I'm gay/lesbian, but there's no way I can talk to them about it." | "Don't be silly.  You're too young to know what you are." |
| | "If they knew I was gay/lesbian, they'd throw me out of the house." | "No child of ours could ever be gay.  I'd disown him/her." |

## Be honest. Questions to ask yourself:

- Do you know how babies are made? (Seriously! You'd be amazed how many kids don't. Or think they do while holding erroneous information such as: "You can't get pregnant the first time." "You can't get pregnant if you do it standing up." "There's no way you can get pregnant if the guy wears a condom." "You can't get pregnant if the girl douches afterwards.")
- Do you feel pressured to have sex by friends, society, your boyfriend or girlfriend?
- Do you use sex as a way to control people or gain power?
- Do you have sex to please others? To feel accepted?
- Are you sexually promiscuous?

***"What does that mean?"***

It means: Do you engage in casual, indiscriminate, and frequent sexual relations, possibly to compensate for feelings of inadequacy?

## Some things to consider:

Sex can be a joyous, meaningful, and rewarding part of life. But unfortunately, AIDS adds a whole new dimension to the issue of teenage sex: DEATH.

Sexual relationships can cause physical, emotional, and psychological damage, depending on the people and the circumstances.

The age of the participants is not necessarily what determines the consequences; many teenagers are more honest, caring, sensitive, and responsible in a sexual relationship than adults. Adolescents, however, because they're experiencing new feelings and situations for the first time, are especially prone to getting hurt or hurting someone else.

At this point in history, with no known cure for AIDS, the consequences of an irresponsible sexual relationship may include dying.

Setting aside moral and religious doctrines that can influence your and your parents' attitudes towards sex, it is impossible to make a judgment on the appropriateness or potential harm of a sexual relationship for a teenager without knowing details about the people involved—their feelings, their levels of maturity and experience, their motivations, their health, their lives.

One thing is certain, though: If you are having sexual relations that put you or your partner at risk for becoming pregnant, or for contracting AIDS or some other sexually transmitted disease, you have just proven your parents right. You *are* too young and immature to have sex.

Only two forms of sex provide 100 percent protection against AIDS and pregnancy:

1. No sex (abstinence), and
2. Sex with yourself (masturbation).

The use of condoms reduces the risk of contracting AIDS and/or becoming pregnant. But sex with condoms, whether anal, oral, or vaginal, whether heterosexual or homosexual, is not "safe" sex. It is "safer" sex. The risk of AIDS still exists, as does the risk of becoming pregnant or getting someone pregnant (although the latter risk can be eliminated, depending on where you put what). Condoms can fail—due to improper use, "wear and tear," defects in manufacturing, or having been squished in a wallet or purse for too long.

Teenagers often have unprotected sex. This can happen because the sex was unplanned, or because judgment has been clouded by drugs or alcohol, or because they don't think "it" can happen to them, or because they think you can't get AIDS or become pregnant from just one time. No wonder the incidence of AIDS is rising faster in teenagers and young adults than in any other segment of the population. No wonder the United States has the highest rate of teenage pregnancy of all industrialized nations.

The issue of teenage sexuality is far too complex to go into here in great detail. Your parents' concerns, however, will tend to be:

1. **Moral:** "It's wrong."
2. **Practical:** "We're afraid you'll get pregnant." "We're afraid you'll get someone pregnant." "We're afraid you'll get AIDS."
3. **Supportive:** "We don't want you to get hurt by having experiences you're not ready for. Don't grow up so fast."

Trust, responsibility, and communication are essential to keeping issues of sexuality from harming your relationship with your parents. These issues are fraught with hidden agendas. Seek them out. Gather intelligence. Identify your parents' specific concerns, fears, and attitudes. Identify yours.

If you and your parents are comfortable talking about sexual matters, use Mom and Dad as resources. They must know *something* about sex. They may be able to give you good advice, help you clarify your own feelings, or see that you have access to condoms, birth control, and/or medical care.

If your parents restrict you in an effort to keep you pure, sit down with them and tell 'em the facts of life. Explain that sex can take place in the afternoon as well as at night. Inform them that sex has been known to occur in cars, in school, in church, in friends' houses, and even in kids' own houses. Educate them to the fact that a 10:00 P.M. curfew isn't going to keep you from having sex. You'll do it at 9:59 P.M., if that's what you really want. Help them to realize that your intelligence, good judgment, and self-control will make you abstain from sex and/or behave responsibly—not their restrictions.

Discovering yourself as a sexual being is one of the projects of adolescence and young adulthood. You deserve the best help you can get. Take a sex ed class, if your school offers one. Read books. Get all the facts about AIDS and sexually transmitted diseases. Talk to trusted adults: school counselors, coaches, teachers, older siblings, doctors, therapists. If they get embarrassed, that's their problem. Try again. You'll find someone you can talk to and trust.

Your friends can be a resource for talking about sex and relationships. You'll discover that you're not alone, that you're not the only person who thinks about sex 428 times a day—or barely thinks about it at all. Be forewarned, though, that your friends (especially the ones who act like they know everything) can be a treasure chest of ignorance, stupidity, and misinformation when it comes to sex. Don't be fooled. Be cautious in accepting what they tell you. Your life and the lives of others are at stake.

## If You Are Gay or Lesbian....

The challenge of coming to terms with your sexual identity may be more difficult for you than it is for heterosexual teenagers. This can happen for several reasons:

- You may not be sure of or willing to accept your sexual orientation.
- You may feel that you have to hide your feelings from your friends, your parents, even yourself.
- You may have heard people say that homosexuality is wrong—a sin, a disease, a perversion.

- You may have experienced or witnessed homophobic prejudice and discrimination.
- People may have threatened you or committed violence against you.
- Your own parents may have made statements that make you feel that they could never accept your sexual orientation.

The discrimination, fear, confusion, and aloneness teenagers who are homosexual may experience places them at higher risk than their heterosexual peers for drug and alcohol abuse and suicide.

If you are a gay or lesbian teenager, I hope that your parents will be as accepting of this aspect of your identity as they are of other aspects. Use the ideas in this book to improve trust and communication so that you can talk about these issues with them. Many bookstores (and certainly gay and lesbian bookstores) carry books that may be helpful. There are books for parents whose children are gay, books that help gay teenagers come out to their parents, books that deal with the feelings and issues gay teenagers must face in their lives.

Try to understand that this is as powerful and emotional an issue for your parents as it is for you. They will respond to your sexuality through the filter of their hopes and expectations for you, their self-image as parents, their feelings, attitudes, and prejudices, their conscious and unconscious desires, their concerns about public reaction, their empathy for the difficulties you may encounter, etc.

As you deal with these issues, both with others and within yourself, here are a few things to keep in mind:

1. There is nothing wrong, sinful, or perverted about you.
2. Homosexual feelings and behaviors have existed in virtually every society and era since the beginning of humankind. Many great figures in history have been homosexual.
3. There is growing scientific evidence that homosexuality is not a "choice," but rather a genetically or biologically based disposition.
4. Gay and lesbian teens are just as capable of leading lives full of love, success, and fulfillment as are heterosexual teenagers.

5.  You deserve all the support you can get in dealing with the feelings and issues you face as a gay teenager.  If you can talk about it with your parents or friends, great.  If not, talk to a school counselor or therapist.  Call a hotline.  You may know some gay adults with whom you would feel comfortable discussing your questions and concerns.  Many cities have support and social groups for gay and lesbian teenagers.  You can learn about these groups through gay newspapers and publications, or from community mental health clinics.

# Inner Space and Outer Limits

## Problems Involving Limits, Restrictions, and Privacy

## The Issue Arena:  Privacy

| Problem | How You See It | How Your Parents See It |
|---|---|---|
| Parents object to your locked door. | "I have a right to my privacy."<br><br>"It's the only way to keep them out." | "It's not safe.  What if there's a fire?"<br><br>"It's our house.  We'll go wherever we please." |
| Parents open your mail. | "They have no right to open my mail or give me the third degree about letters I get." | "We have a right to know what our children are up to." |
| Parents listen in on your phone calls. | "How dare they!!!" | "We want to be sure you're not getting into any trouble." |
| Parents snoop in your bedroom. | "It's my private space. They have no business going in there." | "We're not spying.  We're just cleaning." |
| Parents look through your schoolbooks and assignments. | "Why don't they just ask instead of going through my books and papers?" | "We like to know what you're doing in school."<br><br>"It's the only way we can be sure you're doing your homework." |
| Parents read your diary. | "I have a lot of personal things I don't want them to know about." | "How else can we keep tabs on you?  You never tell us anything." |

## Be honest. Questions to ask yourself:

- Snooping suggests an underlying trust issue. Are you giving your parents any reasons not to trust you?
- Are you sure they're snooping? Could you be paranoid? Could opening your mail be an innocent mistake?
- Do you shut your parents out of your life? Is snooping the only way they have to know what's going on?
- Are you doing things in your room, at school, over the telephone that you shouldn't be doing?

## Some things to consider:

- Find hidden agendas. Are they concerned about drug use behind closed doors? Are they concerned about your social life or sexual activities? Do they feel hurt and left out? Do they not trust your friends?
- If they object to locked doors, try giving them a key for emergency use. Mount an ax in the hall near your door in case of fire. Agree to unlock the door if they'll agree to knock (and wait for an answer) before entering.
- If they open your mail, see if you can get to it first.
  —If they say it's an accident, help them to be more conscious of the fact that some of the mail is yours by putting up your own "mailbox" in the house. Ask your parents to deposit your letters there.
  —If that doesn't work, consider getting a PO box or having people write to you in care of a friend.
- For invasion of telephone privacy, tell your folks how you feel about their snooping and lack of trust. Can you get your own phone line? If necessary, check to be sure that the extension phone has been hung up.
- If your folks can't stay out of your bedroom, tell them how you feel about it. If they say they're "just cleaning," offer to do those chores that bring them into your room.

- For school nosiness, beat them to the punch. Show them your books and work from time to time. Encourage them to talk to your teachers or advisers. Show them you have nothing to hide.

- For diary snooping, seek out hidden agendas. Could it be that you secretly want them to find out certain things? Get in touch with yourself. Are you leaving your diary where it "begs" to be read? Find a better hiding place. If you put your mind to it, there's no way your parents will discover it.

- Recognize that snooping says, "We're trying to find out about you. You never tell us anything. We're not sure we can trust you." One of the best ways to get your parents to stop snooping is to look at the factors that have led to this breach of trust. Find out why they're so suspicious. Address those concerns.

- Tell your parents enough about your life, thoughts, and feelings that they feel they know you. Be sure they realize that it's impossible to have a good relationship with them if they have such little regard for your privacy and personal space. Use I-messages to get your points across.

## The Issue Arena: Where You Can Go, What You Can Do

| Problem | How You See It | How Your Parents See It |
|---|---|---|
| Too many limits and restrictions. | "They treat me like a baby." | "You're not responsible enough." |
| | "They never let me do anything." | "You're too young. It's dangerous." |

## Be honest. Questions to ask yourself:

- Are you responsible?
- Do your parents have cause not to trust you?
- Are you reasonable in what you'd like to do?

## Some things to consider:

- Tell your parents how you feel. Talk about it. Build trust; find out where your parents are getting their impression of you as irresponsible.
- Suggest a trial period or a contract linking your freedom to specific signs of responsibility.
- Identify, with your parents, their particular fears. What steps can you take to address them? Could you go during the day instead of at night? Would it make a difference if you were in a group and not alone? What if you called home to check in?
- Take self-defense classes so your parents won't worry so much.
- Give it time. Lay off the issue for a couple of months. Act responsibly. Then bring your feelings up again.

## The Issue Arena:  Bedtimes

| Problem | How You See It | How Your Parents See It |
|---|---|---|
| Too early. | "I should be able to stay up as late as I want." | "Kids need sleep. You won't be awake for school." |
| | "I can't fall asleep that early." | "We want quiet time for ourselves." |
| | "I'm a night person." | "You make too much noise at night." |

## Be honest.  Questions to ask yourself:

- Are you tired a lot? Do you fall asleep during the day?
- Is your bedtime reasonable for someone your age (even if you don't like it)?
- Do you know the reasons for your parents' position?

## Some things to consider:

- Set up a trial period to see how no bedtime or a later bedtime would affect your energy and schoolwork.
- Make a deal. You can stay up as late as you wish, but you must stay in your room after a certain time.
- Put your siblings to bed in exchange for a later bedtime.
- Shhhh! If you quieted down, they might not even know you're still up.

## The Issue Arena: Curfews

| Problem | How You See It | How Your Parents See It |
|---|---|---|
| Too early. | "I should be able to stay out later." | "You're too young to be out that late." |
| | | "We don't like to have to wait up for you." |
| | "It's not fair. All my friends get to stay out as late as they want." | "Just because their parents let them run wild doesn't mean we're going to." |

## Be honest. Questions to ask yourself:

- When you stay out late, do you come home on time?
- Sure, you'd like to stay out later. Is it reasonable given your age, where you live, others in the household, any burdens it places on your parents as chauffeurs?

## Some things to consider:

- Look for hidden agendas. Perhaps the "early" curfew is because your parents don't trust your friends, fear for your safety, or worry that you'll drink or take drugs if you don't have to encounter them at night. Discover the *real* issue.

- Talk to your parents about their worries and reasoning. Actively Listen. Would they consider changing your curfew if you're not hanging out in a public place? What if you were in a supervised setting or over at a friend's house?

- Use the old alarm-clock trick. This way your parents don't have to wait up for you, but they'll know if you don't get home. Here's how it works: Let's say you have to be in by midnight. Your parents set an alarm clock in their bedroom for 12:00 A.M. It's your job to get home in time to turn it off so they aren't awakened. If you don't, it'll wake them up and they can start to worry. Which means you'd better start to worry, too.

# Mind Your Own Business

## "Why Don't They Just Leave Me Alone?"

## The Issue Arena: Parental Pressures and Expectations

| Problem | How You See It | How Your Parents See It |
|---|---|---|
| Parents nag and criticize everything you do. | "It makes me want to do the opposite, just to show them." | "If you did what we asked, we wouldn't have to nag." |
| Parents are never satisfied with what you do. | "I try the best I can. They want some Superkid and I'm not." | "If you only tried harder, you could do much better." |
| Parents push to make you better, smarter, a higher achiever. | "I can't ever satisfy them. What's the use? They just don't like who I am." | "We expect the best from our children." |

## Be honest. Questions to ask yourself:

- Are *you* satisfied with who you are and what you do?
- If your parents didn't bug you, would you want to change in any of the ways they pressure you to change?
- Are you afraid to be really good at something?
- Do your friends like it when you excel, or do they get jealous or feel threatened?
- Do you ever nag your parents about how *they* are?
- Are your parents' criticisms the only attention you get from them? Do you act up just so you'll be noticed?

## Some things to consider:

- Parents' expectations can be very specific ("We expect an A in chemistry") or broad ("We expect you to show more responsibility").

- Specific expectations lend themselves to problem-solving and troubleshooting strategies (like the ones in Chapters 4 and 5 of this book). You might agree to disagree, engineer a trial period, strike a bargain. Find a specific solution for a specific pressure.

- Broad expectations are trickier. Tell your parents that you don't know what they mean when they say they "expect more responsibility" or "want to see a better attitude." Get them to explain. Actively Listen. Then you'll be in a position to know how you want to respond.

  You might agree with them and decide to try harder. If you disagree, use I-messages to tell them how you feel. Let them know that their pressure and expectations cause hurt, discouragement, or frustration for you. Let them know what you see it doing to your relationship with them.

- Suggest a trial period in which your parents lighten up and let you handle things yourself.

- Get them to stop nagging by doing whatever it is they're nagging you to do.

- Give them a good parenting book that explains why negative pressure is so destructive to kids.

## The Issue Arena:  Homework

| Problem | How You See It | How Your Parents See It |
| --- | --- | --- |
| Parents bug you about doing your homework. | "I wish they'd lay off.  It's my own business." | "If we don't keep after you, it doesn't get done." |
| Parents force you to study. | "It's like boot camp around here.  I can't study if I'm not in the mood." | "If you had the self-discipline to work on your own, we wouldn't have to make you." |
| Parents insist on seeing your work. | "It's my work and I should be able to keep it private." | "We like to know what you're doing in school." |
| Parents want you to get better grades. | "I'm not interested in school.  It's bor-ring." | "If you don't get good grades, you won't go to a good college or get a good job.  It's the path to success." |
| Parents link freedoms to grades. | "It makes me want to flunk just to get back at them." | "We don't like to restrict you, but what else can we do?" |

## Be honest.  Questions to ask yourself:

- Why do your parents bug you about your homework?
- Are you doing poorly in school?
- Are you an academic goof-off?
- Are you lazy?  Bored?  Do you understand the material?
- Is not doing your homework a method you use to get back at your parents?
- Are you afraid to try harder because you might fail?

## Some things to consider:

- If you're doing well in school, your parents have no business bugging you. If you're not doing well in school, their bugging you probably isn't going to help.
- If they force you to study and do your work, you'll never learn to be responsible and self-disciplined yourself.
- Parents should allow and encourage children to deal with their own school problems.
- If you're doing poorly in school, identify why. This will provide clues towards a solution.
  —Do you need a quiet place to work?
  —Do you need tutoring?
  —Do you have a conflict with a teacher?
  —Would changing classes or seats help?
  —Could you study with or enlist the help of a friend?
  —Do you feel okay? Can you see all right?
  —Are you in a terrible and inhumane school?
  —Is poor performance a weapon in your anti-parent arsenal?
  —Are you afraid of being teased or rejected by friends if you do too well?
- Suggest your own ideas for dealing with the problem or improving your performance.
- Poor schoolwork brings with it a set of logical consequences. Repeating a class or grade. Not being able to participate in sports or extracurricular activities. Going to summer school. Closing off options. Ask your folks to allow the "real world" to punish you instead of them.
- Propose a trial period during which your parents stop bugging and you start working on your own.
- Consider changing schools. Do your own research. Present possibilities to your parents. Show them you're motivated. Sometimes it's not that you're a problem child; you're just going to a problem school.

- Beat your parents to the punch. Put a stack of schoolbooks by their bed to look at. Show them an occasional assignment, test, or paper. Keep them informed and they won't have to nag you.
- Tell your folks how their nagging makes you feel. Help them see that your relationship with them would be much more pleasant if school were something between you and your teachers. Think of all the fights and criticism that would disappear.
- Talk to teachers. Make your own proposals. Teachers often admire initiative. Wherever and whenever you can, choose projects that interest you.
- Parents see grades as your route to success (or failure). They might worry less if they see ways in which you are motivated, curious, energetic, productive, and ambitious. Develop talents and interests unrelated to school; these could also be a route to "success."

## The Issue Arena: Attitude

| Problem | How You See It | How Your Parents See It |
|---|---|---|
| Laziness. | "I don't like their attitude either." | "It's not what you do, it's your attitude." |
| Sullenness. | | |
| Disrespect. | | |
| Dishonesty. | | |
| Irresponsibility. | | |
| And on and on.... | | |

## Be honest. Questions to ask yourself:

- Regardless of the reason(s) for your attitude, are your parents correct in their label(s) for it?
- Are you angry? Unlikable? Untrustable? Why?

## Some things to consider:

Attitude issues generally come down to two roots:

1. Problems in style, and/or
2. Problems in the relationship.

*For attitude problems with style roots:*

—Avoid put-downs and threats.

—Put your thoughts and feelings in forms that don't come across as disrespect or "bad attitude."

—Use I-messages. Actively Listen.

—Stay away from your parents when you're in a bad mood.

—Be sure you know specifically what it is in your attitude they don't like. Deal with those issues directly. Are they misinterpreting your behavior? Do they assume you're consciously being "bad" at times when you're not even aware of it? Ask them to define "good attitude."

*For attitude problems with relationship roots:*

—Rebuild trust.

—Use the tricks and treats in Chapter 3 to make your folks feel better.

—Gather intelligence. Seek out hidden agendas.

—Identify your parents' feelings. Do they feel neglected? Unloved?

—Identify what "good attitude" would be to your folks. Then go for it!

# READ THIS LAST!

If you're not reading this part last, no wonder your parents always say:

*"You never do what you're told!"*

However, since you're already here, you might as well join the rest of us, listen to what I have to say, and then take your independent little spirit back to where you belong.

By now, you've had a chance to become acquainted with the many ideas in this book: the nature of parents and teenagers; the importance of trust and responsibility; ways to improve communication, to avoid trouble, to solve problems; ways to bring up parents who will be sensitive and accepting, generous and supportive.

If you're serious about bringing up better parents, this book can work for you. It is my hope and expectation that you'll begin to see positive changes as soon as you put these ideas into practice: fewer fights, fewer tears, more trust, more love, more freedom. Your parents may be as eager as you are to improve family relations. Up to now, they haven't known how to do it. With you leading the way, they just may hop aboard your bandwagon. More people means more momentum; successes multiply, and you'll all be well on your way towards a happier home life.

No matter how great things become, however, there's always going to be that day when everything seems to fall apart. You'll revert to old ways, old habits. You'll have a wing-ding fight that makes you feel like nothing's changed. Your parents will retreat to Parental Authority Positions (P.A.P.), and the new spirit of democracy and respect you so carefully created will go flying out the window along with the vase you threw. When that happens, don't get discouraged. If it took six days (according to some) to create the world, it's bound to take even longer to break patterns and change attitudes that have had years to develop.

Be patient. Don't expect to bat 1000 at the beginning. Right now, you may be hitting only 200; if you can improve your average to 400, you've doubled your success! As long as you and your folks are still on the plus side, you will be able to bring up better parents if you stick with it.

One final thought: Parents being parents, there are going to be times, no matter how hard you try, no matter how reasonable you are, when your folks will be unkind or immature, unreasonable or unfair. They will defy your best efforts regardless of your skill and understanding.

When that happens, there's not much you can do except take comfort in the fact that they'll grow out of it. After all, it's just a stage they're going through.

# INDEX

# About the Author

Very little is known about Alex Packer. His former students describe him as "brilliant," "weird," and "kinda cute." His former teachers are all institutionalized and unavailable for comment. Private investigators hired by the publisher have, however, been able to determine that the author attended Harvard College, where he majored in Social Relations and Late Night Snacks, and that he holds a Master's Degree in Education from the Harvard Graduate School of (duh) Education, as well as a Ph.D. in Educational and Developmental Psychology from Boston College. Underworld informants have told the publisher that Alex Packer was Headmaster of an alternative school for 11-to-15-year-olds, Director of Education at the Capital Children's Museum, and is now president of Boston-based FCD Educational Services, Inc., a leading provider of drug education programs to schools and colleges worldwide.

He is also the author of *365 Ways to Love Your Child* (Dell, 1995), *Parenting One Day at a Time* (Dell, 1996), and *How Rude! The Teenagers' Guide to Good Manners, Proper Behavior, and Not Grossing People Out* (Free Spirit, 1997).

Reliable sources report that Dr. Packer writes screenplays, flies ultralight aircraft, drives a 28-year-old sports car, and lives in a big loft.

When asked to supply a photograph, Dr. Packer refused, saying, "What!?!? And never be able to go out to a restaurant again without hordes of adoring teenagers stampeding to my table for autographs?"